SLEEP
Is for the
WEAK

The best of the mommybloggers including
Amalah, Finslippy, Fussy, Woulda Coulda Shoulda,
Mom-101, and More!

A
BlogHer
Book

Edited by Rita Arens
Foreword by Stacy Morrison, editor of *Redbook*

CHICAGO
REVIEW
PRESS

Library of Congress Cataloging-in-Publication Data

Sleep is for the weak : the best of the mommybloggers including Amalah, Finslippy, Fussy, Woulda Coulda Shoulda, Mom-101, and more : a blogHer book / edited by Rita Arens ; forward by Stacy Morrison.

p. cm.

Includes bibliographical references and index.

ISBN 978-1-55652-772-2 (alk. paper)

1. Motherhood. 2. Parenting. I. Arens, Rita. II. Title.

HQ759.S577 2008

306.874'3--dc22

2008010663

Cover and interior design: Visible Logic

Cover image: Imagezoo/Images.com/Jupiterimages

Published by Chicago Review Press, Incorporated

814 North Franklin Street

Chicago, Illinois 60610

ISBN 978-1-55652-772-2

Printed in the United States of America

5 4 3 2 1

CONTENTS

ACKNOWLEDGMENTS

Special thanks to my husband, Greg; my daughter (the little angel); my parents; my sister, Renee; my best friend, Steph; and Jesus Christ for listening and encouraging me past my anxiety and melodrama to keep this project going. Thanks to Lisa Stone, Jory Des Jardins, and Elisa Camahort Page of BlogHer for all of your professional advice, friendship, and support. Thanks to Liz Gumbinner, Risa Green, Barbara Zitwer, and Esther Chen for your insight into the publishing world. Thanks to Mary Kravenas and Cynthia Sherry of Chicago Review Press for never making me explain what a blog is or why these stories are so important, and for taking a chance on me without an agent. It can be done.

Thanks to all of my contributors, especially Kelli Oliver George, Alice Bradley, Eden Marriott Kennedy, and Jenny Lauck, for thinking the idea was a good one when it was just a baby. Thanks to Heather Armstrong for answering my e-mails and encouraging me when I was about to quit. Thanks to Sarah Lindquist, Becky Brown, Sandee Buller, and Bill Rose, who had to listen to me talk about this book for the past two years at work. Thanks to Bob Stewart and Michael Pritchett for teaching me how to write. Thanks to all of the readers of Surrender, Dorothy, who followed this project and my life with such kindness and interest, even though I don't deserve it. I hope to read you all someday. Keep writing—someone is always reading.

Thanks to the blogosphere for saving me when I was an insane and weepy new mother. I hope now to give something back. All hail Everywoman. All hail Mommy.

FOREWORD

I have a secret.

As far as secrets go, it's not too shocking, dire, or dastardly. But I carry it with a wincing shame nonetheless.

My son—a well-adjusted, social, intelligent, outgoing, confident almost-five-year-old—sleeps in my bed with me. Every night. Every single night. It's not even pretend anymore, as it was all those months when I would tuck him into his bed at night, plant kisses on his sweet face, and pull his door gently closed, knowing full well that he would wake up at 1 A.M. or 2 A.M. or sometimes 11 P.M. and get up out of his bed and pad, pad, pad his way across his room, out the door, turn right, and pad, pad, pad across my floor and climb up into my bed, look at me straight in the face, and say, "OK, Mommy, let's sweep." (His Ls are still a work in development; I will be crushed when he masters them.)

Now I just tuck him right into my bed every night. For a lot of reasons. Because it saves me an hour of screaming and crying that always ends with his being tucked into my bed, anyway. And because I know I have an hour of two of work waiting for me at my dining room table every night, editing the articles that turn into *Redbook* magazine every month. Because I am a working mother who is completely unconflicted about my choice to work, but who has plenty of conflict about how much conflict I can tolerate between me and my

son because of how much time I am away from him, working, traveling, loving my work, and yes, being thrilled to be someone besides
his mother. I guess that's a second secret right there. I am occasionally
thrilled to be someone other than his mother. Sheesh. How terrible
of a person am I? How can I admit these things to myself, much less
anyone else?

But before I break out the ice cream and pour myself a nice, fuzzy
glass of pinot noir to think deeply about these questions—or avoid
thinking about them, perhaps, these failures of self, these frac-
tious, complicated questions of identity and parenthood and guilt
and grace—I have somewhere to go. Online. To dozens, even hundreds—and probably millions, but you know, I have work waiting for
me on the dining room table, so I can't spend too much time tool-
ing around—of stories and thoughts and posts written by women
just exactly like me and not at all like me, women who have made
the same choices or totally opposite choices, women who struggle,
and women who have had one of those rare, gloriously perfect days
where everything came together. They're out there. And in their stories I can find comfort and company and occasionally even a story
that makes my challenges as a single mom with an oversized career
seem quaint, or a story that is so wickedly funny that I laugh and
snort until my sneaky self-loathing has retreated just enough for
me to pull a breath all the way down to the bottom of my lungs and
let it out slowly, feeling calmer, less confused, and certainly not at
all alone.

But the most important thing I find is truth.

As the editor of *Redbook*—a 104-year-old magazine that has seen
many generations of ideas of what a woman's adult life is supposed

to look like—I believe my mission is to help women find their own, individual truths; to give each one permission to hold onto herself, her most private and very best idea of who she is and can become, even as she pours herself into taking care of those around her; to give voice to the hard stuff, because lord knows there is nothing more isolating than thinking you are alone in Hell and everyone else is having a Fucking Great Time.

And what made me believe I could bring this guts and glory to *Redbook* was all the voices I found online, women (and men) telling their hard truths and sharing their moments of transcendence, unpeeling this wildly complicated (and yet incredibly simple) thing called life, one day at a time. All of us are finding our way, and defining our way. Our generation is less suspicious of (and less threatened by) women who aren't like us, and more curious about how they make their lives work. We are connected and supportive, even when we stay anonymous. (Every blog is an iceberg, each single comment representing a mass of silent witnesses.) We learn to have compassion for ourselves and our own failures in reading about other people's failures, because we see how easily we have compassion for them.

And we realize that we are not going crazy. Really. Because every single one of us can't be crazy, right?

Right. We are not crazy. We have simply become the Grown-Ups.

And since I am a grown-up, that means I can decide that it is OK to let my well-adjusted, confident, almost-five-year-old son sleep in my bed. (I figure he'll retreat to his own room and never come out as soon as he figures out the neat things he can do with his penis.) And so instead I choose to celebrate the life I have built for him, for us, by trying not to torture myself about this whole sleeping-in-my-bed thing, and instead making room in my head to really treasure the moments when Zack reaches over to my pillow for my hand and clasps my index finger tight while he sucks noisily on his thumb, his fluttering blond eyelashes grazing his impossibly pink cheek.

The sweet confusion of being the one in charge is a fair price to pay for those moments when your heart is so full that tears squeak out of your eyes.

That's what I find online. That's what I hear from the chorus of voices. That's the lesson that makes me strong, helps me quiet my warring instincts. That's what's captured in this book.

So whether today's a day you're riding the joy train or one that has you shaking your fists at the heavens, pull up a chair. I guarantee you'll find a story from someone just like you, or not at all like you, that will shine a light on something true you didn't even know you needed to know until you found it.

STACY MORRISON
Mom to Zack, 4
www.redbookmag.com/somethingaboutstacy
Editor in Chief, *Redbook*

INTRODUCTION

I read a lot of books while I was pregnant with my daughter in 2003. I thought I knew what to expect. I thought other people would be able to tell me how to be a good parent. I thought my friends and family would understand perfectly how my life had changed.

I was wrong. And I didn't know what to do about that. I didn't know who or what could make me feel better. I wasn't sure if I would ever feel better or normal again.

Eventually, I found the understanding I needed in the blogosphere. There were "mommybloggers" spilling coffee and red wine on keyboards across the world as they recorded their problems—my problems—on their weblogs, or "blogs." Finally—someone who understood exactly what I was afraid of and didn't dismiss or exaggerate my fears.

When I was in graduate school, I took a Victorian literature class with Ms. Jennifer Phegley. She was teaching serial publishing. At the time, I didn't know about blogs, but I remember thinking what a smart thing serial publishing was—how intriguing to get feedback from your readers before you wrote the end of the book, to allow your readers, in some way, to become a part of your plot. That's what attracted me to blogs, particularly mommyblogs. These people wrote nearly every day, they wrote about things that were happening in my life, and they accepted comments and e-mail. They wrote back. They had been where I was. They could help me, and they did. I was so excited by this lifeline from the Internet abyss that I determined I would publish my own story of motherhood, with the hope that my story would help some struggling new mother who came after me. I've been delighted to find this indeed has happened, that there is some circle of life playing itself out in the ether. This book is probably the karmic result of me being honest about sleeping on the floor of my toddler's room for six months straight.

The contributors to this book are also amazing writers, and I do think there can be a difference between "writer" and "blogger." If you want to gain an audience for your blog, just insult someone publicly or create some other virtual trainwreck. If you want to keep an audience (and these writers aren't short on readers by any stretch of the imagination), you have to be consistently witty, poignant, or some combination of the two. You have to string together good sentences day after day. It takes stamina. The women and one man who contributed to this book are indeed writers, and writers of such a caliber that I'm honored to call them my colleagues and friends. Not pleased, honored.

When my daughter was two, I decided to compile a collection of the best of mommyblogging into a book that I could give her when she someday had her own child. I figured it was the nicest thing that I could do as her mother, because I'd seen firsthand how quickly we forget the pain part of parenthood. As I thought about it, I realized other mothers (and fathers) might need this book as badly as she would.

The project got a little out of hand.

So now, I present to you and to her a book to remind you that it does get better: *Sleep Is for the Weak*. (And hey, it does get better.)

1

Not Understanding the Rules

Whether or not we realize it, there are rules involved with being a parent. Rules for how we'll discipline our kids, rules for how we'll behave in front of them, rules for how we'll interact with other adults, childless or childful. You think you understand them until that's your adorable offspring throwing a tantrum in a crowded restaurant, your child begging for candy in the checkout line, your best friend who's suddenly furious you canceled a dinner date with her because you haven't slept more than two hours a night in three weeks. It's only then that you realize: you never really understood the rules before.

WHEN TODDLERS RULE

Alice Bradley FINSLIPPY

Dear prospective parent,

Thank you for considering parenting me. As my current situation is somewhat wanting, I am, as you know, looking for a new arrangement. Below is a list of my demands.

I. FOOD

1. For BREAKFAST, there will be only MILK from my SIPPY CUP while watching TELEVISION (see section II).
2. From BREAKFAST until what you probably call LUNCH, I will be provided with an unending supply of cookies. No arguments.
3. For LUNCH, I will eat YOGURT. Anything with FRUIT ON THE BOTTOM will make me pick out the fruit and throw it on the ground, or else throw it up on your carpet.
    a. So no FRUIT ON THE BOTTOM.
4. From LUNCH until DINNER, I enjoy having something to lick. Why not a LOLLIPOP? Why not seven?
    a. Between licks, I may place the LOLLIPOP upon your grandmother's Turkish rug. This will be OK by you.
5. For DINNER, I will have MACARONI AND CHEESE. Any attempts to offer me vegetables in addition to the macaroni and cheese will result in TEARS.

    a. And don't you dare hide anything in the cheese sauce, because my God, how you will RUE THE DAY.

6. After dinner, you may provide me with ICE CREAM.

    a. No frozen yogurt—I know the DIFFERENCE.

II. TELEVISION

1. Will be on ALL THE TIME, unless I say differently. While watching TELEVISION, you are to sit by my side, quietly, hands folded in lap, whilst I enjoy my shows.

    a. You may arise to fetch me a SNACK or a DRINK.

2. No DIAPER CHANGING or PLEAS TO ENGAGE IN PHYSICAL ACTIVITY will be tolerated during the watching of the TELEVISION.

3. Turning off of the TELEVISION will result in much SCREAMING.

III. TOYS

1. There will be many.

    a. They will always be strewn about the house so that I may simply reach down and pick up a toy, no matter where I am.

    b. They will be loud, complicated, and contain many small bits. I enjoy the SHOOTING NOISES that go *w-shooooop* or *zim zim zim*.

    c. Nothing that results in LEARNING, please.

IV. FRIENDS

1. Should be available should I be in the mood to use someone else's TOYS or ingest someone else's COOKIES.

    a. They may not ever so much as look at my toys or cookie supply.

    b. Ever, ever, ever.

V. SLEEP

1. Is when I say, where I say, and how I say. If I want to sleep UPSIDE DOWN with my legs locked around your neck, then that's how it will be.

   a. And you will enjoy it.

VI. AFFECTION

1. Occasionally I enjoy being hugged and kissed. I stress OCCASIONALLY.
2. I will not be pelted with wet-mouthed assaults on an hourly basis. Should you feel the need to HUG or KISS, you must provide me with a written request, and then wait for me to offer you my pudgy cheeks.
3. Should I feel the need to be HUGGED and KISSED or SERENADED by my original "parents," I reserve the right to call them and have them come over, just for the HUGGING and the KISSING and maybe a SONG.

   a. After that, it's vamoose, bozos, you had your chance.

THE THINGS THEY NEVER TOLD ME

Izzy Dean IZZYMOM

On numerous occasions in the past six years, I have pondered the curious nature of the clubs to which I now belong, which are the parenthood club and the motherhood club. I'm not even really sure that "club" is the right word. Maybe "secret society" is more befitting. I say that because until you join these clubs, there are things that you will not know and that nobody will ever dare tell you.

For example, when you ask someone how they are enjoying their new status as a parent or how they like having a new baby, they never *ever* tell you that it's ass-kickingly hard work and that you will never, ever own your life again, or that you will be dead tired for the first year, particularly if you're the mother. No, they tell you all the good stuff. It's wonderful. They're so fulfilled. They can't imagine their lives without their child. It's all good! And then they start working on you to join the club.

Now, I'm not saying that all those good things about parenthood aren't 100 percent true for me. They are. But honestly, it's kind of like false advertising to not share some of the downsides if someone is asking you about it. But they never do! And it's not just limited to the experience of having a new baby. Nooooooo! They hold out on all sorts of important things that would have helped me immensely.

An example? OK, how about hemorrhoids? I mean, sure, they briefly mention the H word in that book that *everyone* gets when she's pregnant for the first time. But *nobody* tells you the cold, hard truth about them, which is that once you have them, it's entirely possible they'll *never* go away.

Nor do they tell you that if your husband is at your side during delivery he might actually *see* you *get* your hemorrhoids. Yeah, I know, it's really funny when it's not you! But see, that's what happened to me. And then a nurse counted them for me. "You have one, two, three, four little hemis!" My God, she made them sound so darn cute. But seventeen months later? They're not so cute, and I've pretty much given up all hope of those adorable little guys ever vacating my utterly humiliated butt.

See, they make you *think* they're gone, and then one day you're very innocently doing your business without any excessive pushing (because I'm now well trained in how not to poop), and you feel that familiar prickly sensation and you know they never really left.

As if the "hemis" weren't bad enough, there's the whole incontinence issue. Seriously, I have never, ever been told or even gotten the impression that pushing out a baby is going to very possibly make you leak pee for the rest of your life whenever you sneeze, cough, get up off the floor too quickly, or jump on a trampoline. Nobody tells you that!

I honestly thought that all those Serenity and Poise pad commercials were for senior citizens, and I'd be all, "Why do they have these attractive young women in the commercials? That's so stupid!" Seriously, I thought that shit was for *old* people.

Well, let me tell you, long after being discharged from the hospital, *months* later in fact, I was still buying Poise pads by the damn case, and I frequently considered how my fellow club members never uttered a word about this. Now, to be fair, maybe they had normal labors (mine was thirty-six hours) and pushed for less time (I pushed for almost three hours) and delivered smaller babies (I gave birth to a toddler) and didn't experience the hemis and incontinence. But still, someone out there knew about this and didn't tell me!

But honestly, I think the worst half-truth of all, a veritable lie of omission, is the notion perpetuated by nearly everyone that you will have a baby, get a touch of the "baby blues," get over it, and be blissfully happy forever thereafter. That's the biggest load of shit ever, and frankly, it gives me chills to think of how brutal real postpartum depression actually is.

I suffered from it with my first child, and all I can say is "Baby blues, my ass." There is nothing in the world that could have prepared me for what lay ahead as I went about the business of getting ready for my baby to be born. I was blissfully ignorant of PPD and all the other things that nobody tells you about.

Like colic.

Christ on a crutch, why didn't anyone tell me a baby could scream for more than six hours solid without so much as a thirty-second intermission?

I would call our pediatrician, and he would say, "Babies cry. They all have a fussy time in the evening." And I would growl into the phone, "But it's freaking two in the afternoon!"

My mother-in-law would tell all her church circle friends about the screaming, and of course they all had *the* miracle solution that was going to keep me from walking in front of a bus and cure the colic.

Let's see, there was the "football hold" that made me feel like the screaming baby would just roll right off my arm on to the floor and scream even more when she cracked her head open. Pass.

And the colic "gripe water" that we drove forty-five minutes to go buy. It smelled like pickle juice! I *hate* pickles! No wonder the baby gagged when I tried to give her even the teensiest bit of it. Pass.

Oh, and I can't forget the time my husband and I were strolling with the screaming baby, hoping the motion would lull her to sleep. It didn't. She howled and screeched the entire time, and it was so damned loud, such an unholy racket, that this kindly old lady came out of her house and approached us to "see if the baby was OK."

No. She's mortally wounded, but we thought we'd take a quick cruise around the block before taking her to the ER.

But seriously, I think if the nice old lady had offered to *take* the baby for an hour or two, I would have handed her over immediately.

Because of PPD-related insomnia, I spent my nights rocking the baby and sobbing, wondering why on earth I had thought this whole thing was a good idea. I really felt duped, like I was the butt of some cosmic joke where everyone in the known universe agreed to not tell me that real babies are never like the ones in Gerber commercials and the moms are *never* as happy as they are on TV. Ha ha. Not funny.

I was convinced that the baby cried so much because of me. That I was a bad mother, that I was ill-prepared, that something I was doing or not doing was the cause of all our problems. It didn't help that the pediatrician said my daughter cried because she sensed my nervousness—to which I would reply that I wouldn't be so nervous if she didn't cry so much.

Either way, I just hated life so much. I did not, however, hate the baby. I loved her. I knew I loved her. But I have to confess that it was so frightening and devastating to not be able to "feel" it. I knew it was there, and I was always reaching inside myself to try to grasp it. But the depression just numbed my spirit so much, I couldn't.

And I also feared I would shake her because of the colicky crying. On more than one occasion, I would walk across the house with my arms outstretched in front of me, taut and unbending so I couldn't move them, and carry her to her crib. I knew she would be safe in there while I tried to compose myself and quell the volcano of emotions I knew were on the verge of erupting if I didn't get a grip.

It wasn't just anger, though. It was hopelessness, evidenced by the day my husband came home to find me crying in an inconsolable heap on the floor. Another day I went to a childhood resource center and begged them to help me as I sobbed uncontrollably in their doorway.

Perhaps now you can understand why I feel it's unconscionable to downplay the "baby blues." And colic. My God, anyone who says colic is just an upset tummy should be publicly flogged. That was one of the worst experiences of my life, and I'll be damned if it was because of an "upset tummy."

But take heart—my story of maternal ignorance and woe does get better.

You see, four months into my hellish experience known as early motherhood, another pediatrician suggested we try my daughter on some Zantac for acid reflux. Wonder of wonders, it worked. Within a couple weeks, she was a different child. The screaming was reduced to a normal level, and I was finally able to stop Googling "incessant crying" and "baby screams like a feral cat" in search of clues for what was wrong with her.

Not long after that, she started to sleep through the night, and very slowly my depression started to lift until one day I woke up and realized I felt hopeful again. The future might actually be good. Most importantly, I felt the love, the love I knew was there all along.

These days, when I discuss being a parent with someone who is expecting or trying to get pregnant, I'm always brutally honest about the harder aspects of having a child. The great irony of it all is that nobody really wants to hear it. And in my heart of hearts, I can't blame them at all. Ignorance really is bliss.

VACATIONING WITH CHILDLESS PEOPLE

Rita Arens SURRENDER, DOROTHY

This afternoon I will pack up the little angel, my suitcase, my beloved's suitcase, the little angel's suitcase, the little angel's inflatable bed, pillows for everyone, Tad the Singing Frog, Sluggerrr, books, coloring books, stickers, toys, an inflatable swimming pool, sixty-four bottles of water, and various other accoutrements to pick up my beloved and join six friends, two of them single and childless, for a weekend at a lake.

It's supposed to be sixty-two degrees and raining on Saturday. A good time to review the rules for vacationing with childless people.

Parent Rules:
- I will remove all the batteries from the toys that make noise.
- I will bring a protective sheet for the table, and washable crayons.
- I will bring a portable DVD player so the main television is not taken over by Thomas, Nemo, or any other celebrity-voiced, animated character.
- I will put all used diapers in a trash can outside. I will resist the urge to change the little angel's poopy diaper in front of other people, especially if they are eating.
- I will not discuss my child's bodily functions.
- I will have at least one conversation per day during which my attention is not diverted the entire time.

- I will not inquire into their childbearing or marital plans.
- I will not read *Parenting* magazine.
- I will not lament the cost of babysitters or daycare.
- I will not sing "The Wheels on the Bus" during drinking games.
- I will not insist they talk to my daughter on the phone on the way there.
- I will not leave her in their care while I go skinny dipping (unless they volunteer).

I was well aware of the rules for parents before I became a parent, just as I was judgmental of those horrible parents yelling at their children in the grocery store and letting them eat ice cream for breakfast. The nerve of those people, I thought. *I will never become them.*

Ha.

But as I became a parent, I forgot the rules. I changed my newborn's poopy diaper on my best friend's brand-new granite kitchen counter. I ask people if they want to talk to my daughter on the phone all the time. While pregnant, I bitched incessantly about being pregnant. I now have to constantly remind myself that not everyone wants to hear every blessed detail about my life as a parent.

However, I will, of course, expect the childless people to follow their rules.

Childless People Rules:
- They will not expect my two-year-old to be well behaved at all times.
- They will not expect her to chew with her mouth closed or eat healthy foods.

- They will not expect her to remain a happy girl after her bedtime or stay up partying until midnight at the dinner location of their choice.
- They will not expect my full attention when the little angel is near sharp corners, open water, or animals bearing pointy teeth or claws.
- They will not tell stories of how bad other parents are when I do the same things in their presence.
- They will respect my child's need for naps and excuse us from activities that take place during those naps.
- They will not encourage me to drug my child so that she will go to sleep.
- They will place breakable objects, pointy things, beer cans, and medicine on high shelves or counter tops and not right on the damn floor.
- They will keep in mind that I was once one of them and have not completely lost my mind along with my privacy, money, and flat stomach.

NOTES FOR AMELIORATION

Tracey Gaughran-Perez SWEETNEY

Yesterday I told my daughter I loved her and waited for the expected "I love you, Mommy," to be voiced in return. When this wasn't forthcoming (perhaps she didn't hear me?), I went so far as to ask her directly, like an idiot, "Do you love Mommy?"

She looked at me—her face completely expressionless—and said flatly, "No."

Thus began several minutes of good-natured but increasingly pathetic and desperate cajoling on my part. *Oh, of course you love Mommy! Mommy loves you, so you love Mommy, right?* And still she shook her head slowly, squeaking no at each slightly rephrased query.

Now of course I know she didn't mean it. Of course I know that at two-and-a-half years of age she doesn't even fully comprehend the significance, power, or even the full meaning of love, or of her repeated denials. But regardless, for all my feigning of maturity and knowing better, that shit *hurts*. To have your child—the default center of your emotional universe, for whom you labor and worry and do all kinds of unpleasant, frustrating, and generally bullshit things for the sake of—emphatically deny you of what, at bottom, makes all the hard and exhausting work of parenting rewarding and worthwhile, well, it's kind of a hard pill to swallow. At some point in all of this back and forth with my daughter something in me just sort of *broke.* I got up, went into the bathroom, shut the door, and cried as quietly as I could.

Somewhere there is a lesson here, and it's something I'm still trying really hard to accept and incorporate into my emotional lexicon: unconditional love requires some kind of maturity I don't yet possess but that I really need to work at acquiring. Because the truth is that my daughter doesn't have to love me (though, yes, I know that she does), but I do indeed love her and *that* is what matters. Her returning my feelings is a bonus, but it is not compulsory.

In a broader sense, this rule is applicable to all relationships and circumstances: sometimes we care for people who cannot or do not return the feeling, but the fact that they don't should not negate what we feel. Sometimes we care for people who are broken in ways that render them incapable of it, or they lack a different kind of maturity—the kind that allows for love—or maybe they're just shits who don't care for anyone but themselves. No matter, we can and should still care for them, so long as we do so without expectation, knowing full well that we may only be disappointed or hurt in return.

To have the feeling of love, in and of itself, be enough, to revel in the miraculous existence of deep feeling for another human in a world so often cold and devoid of care, I want to get to that place— to be *that big of a person.* I know I'm far from it, still wearing as I am the old and new scars of my heart on my sleeve and all-too-studiously nursing wounds of disaffection and lack.

2

Never Sleeping Again

Everyone has an Achilles heel, and mine is sleep. Take away my alarm clock, and I can easily sleep ten to twelve hours. My natural rhythm calls for nine full hours. Before my daughter entered my life, I usually got around eight. Now I'm lucky to get six—and there was a period when she was between eighteen and twenty-four months old that I was getting around five broken hours of sleep a night. And working full-time outside the home.

After about six months of this torture—and it was torture—I found myself crying about two hours a day, doing frantic Google searches for sleep solutions. I read every book on sleep there was to read. Nothing worked. I eventually sought out a psychiatrist who put me on some medication to help me not want to kill people because of my constant exhaustion (even if I still wasn't sleeping). Even now that my daughter is four years old, I still find myself called from dreamland at least three times a week. For me, learning to adjust to less sleep has been the single hardest challenge of motherhood. Anyone who tells you their kid sleeps perfectly is either lying or, well, lying.

SLEEPING ON THE FLOOR

Amy Jo Jones BINKYTOWN

Can you think of anything better than lying in the dark, having a sweet conversation with your twenty-one-month-old whose language skills are budding right before your eyes? (OK, not exactly, because it's dark, but you know what I mean.) Stringing together adorable little fragments of sentences? I can. Most days I would tell you something better would be having that conversation at ten o'clock in the morning instead of at four.

Last night I had about five hours of sleep: two on the couch, two in my bed, and one on the floor, the very cold, hard floor, wrapped in a blanket next to my son's crib. Call me crazy, but I would rather lie there listening to him recite sweet nothings about trucks and cars and pumpkins at that ungodly hour than lie in my own bed listening to him wail and scream with a pillow over my head, the whole time wishing we were all asleep. Note to new moms: Those baby books people give you about sleep? They are for babies. Notice how no one bought you one for toddlers? You see, it's because when they are toddlers NOTHING WORKS.

Everybody knows what you are in for when you have a baby. Babies don't sleep. Got it. Of course I was exhausted, but even during the most difficult of days, I managed to find a rhythm. I could let the dog out, feed the baby, take my vitamins, and change my pajamas while sitting on the toilet, all without regaining full consciousness, able to collapse into my unmade bed for a few more hours of slumber. Even after going back to work, I wore my disheveled look with pride. I would tell people I had been up since four, not to exhort sympathy, but because I was amazed that I could function, managing to get to work with matching shoes on under those circumstances, much less accomplish it for months on end.

I thought by now, with my son at almost two years of age, sleep would be a nonissue, and I'd be devoting more of my spot-on mothering skills to making sure he wasn't eating dog food (which he has) and giving himself black eyes from overzealous flopping about on the furniture (he's also done that). I was wrong. (Obviously.)

There were times in the early stages when I actually enjoyed being awake during the dark, quiet four o'clock winter hours when everything was silent—much like a little kid when staying up past her bed time. It was as if more of the world was mine for an hour or two because no one else was around to see it. Not anymore.

Despite the fact that many other moms have thrown the old all-encompassing "this too shall pass" at me, and the pediatrician assures me that one day he will be a teenager and I'll never be able to get him out of bed, I don't think I will ever sleep again.

What will I do when he no longer looks to me to see if touching the television after being told not to seven hundred times is really not a good idea? When he stops believing me that anything with a slight amount of texture is really a tasty piece of cheese and unquestioningly pops it in his mouth? What about the super scary stuff like when girls start to call, or when he wants to go on a camping trip with his friends or the senior trip to Scotland without me? When he wants to test his independence in ways that don't include flopping on the floor or stomping his feet?

This morning he called for me at four thirty. I tried my lying down on the floor trick, but he just wasn't having it. After a few minutes I picked him up, not entirely sure what I should do with him once I did: Walk around until he settled down? Lay him down in his crib and let him cry it out? Bring him to our bed, ensuring everyone would be up for the day and leaving no chance for any more sleep?

As I held him close, the crying subsided, so I stood still. I felt his body relax into mine.

I asked him, "Do you want to lie with me?"

"Lie with me?" He repeated—his way of answering yes.

We got on the floor, on the rug next to his crib. I fluffed up the pillow, and we shared my blanket. His hands felt a little cold, so I covered his up with mine, and we snuggled up in the quiet darkness. I didn't think about what time it was or how much I had to do today. All I could think about was how perfect it felt to have my busybody toddler content to lay peacefully next to me, his little fingers wrapped around mine.

As his breathing deepened and he became relaxed, I sensed sleep was near. A few minutes passed, and I reluctantly tried inching my hand away so as not to disturb him.

"Mama?" he said. He was still awake.

"Yes, baby. I'm right here."

"Hold hands?" he asked.

"Sure, baby. Let's hold hands."

He again wrapped his little fingers around my hand and with it, my heart.

I thought to myself, *I would trade a lifetime of sleep for this.*

IS IT POSSIBLE TO MAIL ORDER SOME PEACE AND QUIET?

Susan Wagner FRIDAY PLAYDATE

I love Charlie, I really do. From the very first moment of his little life, he has been my easy baby. He slept through the night at two months. He has always slept in his own bed. He has always taken a good nap. But recently, not so much.

We are people of routine—which is good, as the first thing parents are told about ADHD kids is "Routine is so important!" I heard that when Henry was diagnosed, and I thought, "Well crap, I don't know how much more routine we can work into our routine, but we'll try." Wade and I both function better when the day follows a predictable pattern, and we realized very early on that we would be better parents if we had a good routine for the boys. We are also people who need both sleep and personal time—two things that go out the window when the baby comes home. But we have worked hard over the past five years to establish useful routines for eating and bathing and sleeping, and until now, it has all worked well.

For the last while, our evenings have gone like this: We eat, usually all together. I clean up the kitchen while Wade has some time with the boys. He plays with them, supervises their bath, and then reads to them for a while. We take turns snuggling with each child (the boys have separate rooms, for so many reasons). And then!

Sleep! And adult conversation! And the occasional nookie. Or television, whatever seems sexier.

Recently, though, Charlie has decided that this whole bedtime thing just isn't working for him and that he should spend the forty-five minutes after we tuck him in repeatedly getting out of bed and wandering around the house. Because clearly he is not ready to sleep. This is annoying, to say the least, as he has been seriously disrupting my trash TV watching. (Really, you are compelled to turn anything on MTV off when your three-year-old comes in the room, don't you think?)

There are a number of issues here. First is the Daddy Time. Despite my suggestions/warnings/demands that this be a *quiet* playtime (as it comes both right before bed and at the end of Henry's long napless day, when he is the most on edge), Wade likes to play Dragon Hunter and Hide and Seek and Hallway Bowling with the boys. And yes, I do appreciate his enthusiasm and energy, but by 6:30 on any given weeknight, I've had it with the running and yelling and crashing into things. And the crying—don't even get me started on the crying.

Then there is the bath. After a rousing game of Jump Out and Yell Boo, Wade expects the boys to settle peacefully into the tub and *not* splash or throw toys or do anything. Which, as I try *so very hard* NOT to point out to him (every single night) is too much to expect from *normal* kids, never mind *our* kids. And so the bath is wild and stressful. Henry nearly always hits his head on the spigot, Charlie cries about something, Wade ends up yelling, and I need a drink.

Then there is the reading. Henry has been wanting to read the Harry Potter books, which we love, but they are a bit over Charlie's head (too much plot, too many characters, too many big words, too few pictures of dinosaurs). So he spends Story Time jumping off Henry's bed, which makes everyone mad.

We have, as you might imagine, made a few adjustments to the routine. I'm making no headway whatsoever with the Wild Daddy Games part of the evening, but I have been able to convince Wade that giving the boys their baths separately is much less stressful. We also realized, just a few days ago, that Charlie really needs his own Story Time, with books he likes and the full attention of one parent. And, despite the fact that most of this was indeed my idea, I feel compelled to say it's working like a charm.

Except for Charlie and the wandering around. He is less likely to wander if he has had a nice long snuggle before he is tucked in, but the real problem seems to be that he just isn't tired, at least not at the same moment Henry is. By 7:30, Henry is done in, especially when he has been at school all day. And the medication seems to be wearing him out at the end of the day, too. Tonight he could barely keep his eyes open while we were reading. I tuck him in and typically don't hear from him until nearly 7:00 A.M.

Charlie, on the other hand, had a nap today of maybe an hour, which was apparently enough to stoke him for some all-night pre-school partying. At 8:00, when Henry was snoozing away, Charlie was jumping on his bed. Literally. In the dark, just jumping and bumping into the wall and laughing! How cute it would have been if I hadn't wanted to sell him on eBay at that very moment. Of course, the jumping on the bed was better than the no less than eight times that he came pattering out of his room announcing, "Mommy, I *need something.*"

I'm thinking that the problem may be the nap. And that we may have to—gulp—*give up the nap.* Which may kill me. The hour during the afternoon when the boys are "resting" is the only thing standing between me and a padded room. It's often the only time during the day when someone is not talking to me. On the other hand, this bedtime thing leaves me completely stressed out at, well, bedtime, which is not good for a chronic insomniac like me. So I'm trying to see it as a trade-off.

The problem is that I need some time for myself. I *need something*.

SLEEP CYCLES

Rita Arens SURRENDER, DOROTHY

Bring me your tired, your exhausted, your red-eyed, bed-headed disasters. Lie down here next to me, darling, and I'll tell you a story. Herein lies the real sleep cycle of adulthood.

1) **Alcohol-Induced.** Typically occurs following a night you spent partying when you knew damn well you had to get up early to see your grandmother, go to work, or graduate from college. Usually accompanied by a hangover, this type of tired can be eliminated simply by going to bed early the next night or napping after whatever you had to do at 7 A.M. ends. *Sympathy level: 1 Pillow.*

2) **Insomnia-Related.** Sometimes, you just can't sleep during the night because your feverish brain is cataloging the Internet, creating voodoo dolls of your boss, or worrying you may never, ever get married and have a family. Sleep often comes along like a freight train about an hour before you have to get up for the day. You wake by force and feel shitty and groggy until about noon. Sleep aids and caffeine avoidance (and sometimes a good therapist) can help alleviate this type. *Sympathy level: 4 Pillows.*

3) **The Love Bug.** You're having so much hot sex you don't have time for sleep. Waking is not an issue, because there can be more sex. You're carried through the day by adrenaline and the thought of yet more sex. Sex, sex. You're in love. We all hate you. *Sympathy level: 1 Pillow.*

4) **New-Baby-Induced.** The child, he eats every hour and a half. And you, poor woman, are the bottle. You were not expecting this level of crazy. You drag yourself, however, almost cheerfully out of bed every hour and a half, because you are so damn happy the baby is still alive—you never thought it possible!—and you are still sort of medicated with some good narcotic shit they gave you in the hospital. Sometimes this type can be combined with #2, and this is a very bad thing. However, most of society expects you will be in this condition and you are usually not required to go to the office, both Good Things. *Sympathy level: 5 Pillows.*

5) **Toddler-Induced.** Sometimes the toddler will successfully sleep through the night for months on end as a baby, lulling you into a sense of false security that you have birthed an angel baby, a good sleeper. Then, inexplicably, the toddler begins waking up every hour on the hour for no reason at all. The child is not sick. The child is not in pain. The child is not hungry. The child is just awake and crying, and you sort of want to move next door so that you do not have to listen anymore. You no longer care that the child is flesh of your flesh, you just want the child to go hibernate for a few years so that you can catch up on your sleep. Everyone expects that you would've Ferbered your child into sleeping by now, so you must therefore be doing something wrong to bring this wrath of nonsleep upon yourself. Oh, and you're back at work and have been for over a year. *Sympathy level: 1 Pillow.* Fuck.

TO SLEEP, PERCHANCE, OR MAYBE NOT

Sheryl Naimark PAPER NAPKIN

Tonight Emily and Haley are having a friend sleep over. Maybe that means I will only have to share the bed with Aaron tonight. My house is almost as active at night as it is during the day, as we all play a rousing game of musical beds all night long. I have nothing against "family beds"—hey, whatever works for you—but I always wanted my kids to sleep in their own beds.

They had other ideas. We put a mattress on the floor right next to our bed so that, if our kids wake up in the night, they can come in and sleep next to us. We brought them in and introduced them to the mattress.

"Children, meet the mattress. Mattress, these are the children. If you have a bad dream or need to be near us, please feel free to slumber on this lovely mattress. This one, down here, on the floor. Doesn't it look comfy?"

Naturally, they get in our bed until we are packed in like sardines. At that time, I transfer myself to the floor. Good thing we have that mattress down there, or I'd never get any sleep. Eventually, they each wake up and say, "Hey, would you look at that? Mom's down there on the floor. She must be lonely sleeping all by herself."

So first one and then the other join me, until I'm completely smooshed. Sometimes I move into their bedroom until finally the sun rises and our little game of nocturnal tag is over.

I was adamant about not transferring Will from his crib into a bed until we got a king-size bed. But lately he wakes up and ever so quietly calls to me, "Mother, mother? Are you awake, Mother, dear? I hate to put you out, but if it isn't too terribly troublesome, would you mind awfully if I slept with you for the rest of the night?"

Sometimes I pull him into bed with us. We snuggle and he's quiet for a moment and then he lifts his leg . . . and drops it. Lifts his leg . . . and drops it. Lifts his leg . . . and drops it. Uh, son, I'm glad all your limbs are in proper working order, but would you mind testing your theories on gravity when it's *daytime*?

And sleeping with Haley is like wrestling with an alligator. She flails hither and yon like she's dreaming the fight scenes in an adventure movie with a few princesses thrown in. Anyway, I know it's just a phase and that in a few years I'll wish I still had night visitors.

Or maybe not.

3

Diapers, Potties, and Upholstery

Potty training is one of the most disgusting and loving acts a parent can commit. It seems potty training is also the only memory not erased by time. Even parents with grandchildren remember the smell of that first solid-food-filled diaper, the time the potty-training toddler released a fecal explosion onto the upholstered couch, the value of hardwood floors. You really have to love someone to wipe his or her ass.

SEND IN THE NEGOTIATOR

Jenny Lauck THREE KID CIRCUS

Potty training my youngest is about as far down on the list of fun as a bulleted item can get.

One morning, she chirped, "Mommy! I need peeps! I use paaaaawty." I might have done a little jig, I'm not certain. I hustled her to the bathroom, and with much fanfare, seated her royal hein-ass on the Dora the Explorer toilet seat.

She beamed at me. I sat across from her on the storage bench. A minute went by, with no peeps.

"Honey, you got peeps? Show Mama."

"Yes. Peeps." (Makes *pissssss* sound with her mouth.)

"Uh, no. Why don't we sit here for a minute and see if you can make *real* peeps."

"OK!" We sit in expectant silence. She makes the *pisssssss* sound again.

"Well, yes. That's what it will sound like, but let's try for some real peeps, OK?"

"Hey! I want my duck!"

And so began the longest ninety minutes of my potty-training career. After handing her the duck, I was informed that I needed to play pirates and mermaids using a plastic rowboat, a rubber dino-saur, a doll missing her head, and an empty toilet paper roll.

After a few minutes of "Yo ho ho!" and "Aaargh!" I suggested some books to pass the time, until she made peeps.

I fetched a book that had a duck with a squeaker embedded in it and read it once. And again. And again. And again. On the tenth go-round, I decided a glass of juice might get things moving, and another book. A person can only quack so many times in one day.

I provided juice. I provided entertainment. I gave her my undivided attention and she gave me zilch. We even played a game that involved my knees talking to her knees.

I was a potty hostage, and I kept thinking if I befriended my captor, I just might make it out of there.

Bah! Heh! Hee! Hoo! Hmm.

No.

Of course, my stubborn streak said to keep sitting there. She hadn't gone yet and she'd had nine hundred gallons of juice, two varieties even, and it had been at least an hour. I had to pee just thinking about that, so surely it would happen any second. She was delighted to be sitting there, wasn't making a move to get down.

I sang "The Wheels on the Bus" with a potty theme. The handle on the toilet goes up and down, the water in the bowl goes 'round and 'round, the pee pee in the potty goes tinkle, tinkle . . .

Shakes fists at parenting gods, who are smirking and alternately pointing at me and making pisssssssss *noises behind their hands.*

At the ninety-minute mark, I really had to pee myself, so I thought a demonstration would be in order. I lifted my little camel off the potty seat and said, "OK, honey, watch Mommy!" (It was really an audio-only program, given the size of Mommy and the reduced dimensions of the Dora seat.)

As soon as I started to go, she got the Look. You know, the Aha! Look. She immediately hightailed it to the living room, leaving me frantically trying to finish going so that I could successfully potty train my child.

Ah, the sound of a full bladder being emptied onto laminate flooring. And then, splashing.

I raced down the hall, pants around my ankles, swooped up my daughter (who was doing the Mexican Hat Dance in her puddle) half screaming, half whining, "No, no, no, no, no, *no!*" in a pinched voice. I enlisted the hubs to clean up the pee while I carried my clapping and "Hurray!" shouting daughter back to the bathroom to clean her up.

Is there a lesson in this? I can tell you that I have trained my daughter to believe that if she wants my attention or a story or whatever, she can claim to want to use the potty, and I will drop everything and sit there putting on five-star entertainment like a suckah.

WHO SAYS HAVING A POTTY-TRAINED KID IS EASIER?

Stefania Pomponi Butler CITYMAMA

I'm ashamed to admit it, but I miss diapers.

At least with diapers, if you don't *feel* like changing it right that second, you can let your kid sit a little while. You don't have to spring up from whatever you are doing to run to the toilet.

You don't have to get splashed with nasty-ass, pee-poo water as you empty the contents of the potty chair into the toilet.

You don't have to plunge the toilet almost daily from all the toilet paper being sent down it. When Bunny is on the big toilet, the toilet paper is unrolled directly into the toilet in one continuous stream, bypassing her bits completely.

You don't have to listen to your kid say they "hafto pee" ten skillion times when they are supposed to be in bed.

You don't have to stand patiently waiting for your child to decide which animal her scat looks like today (fish, snake, or seal), then applaud her choice and agree with her that it does look like it is swimming in a yellow lake.

You don't have to declare the living room sofa a biohazard area after your child gets up off the potty without telling you, then decides to go perform some Fosbury Flops on the couch.

Yes, I miss diapers.

WARNING: THIS IS REALLY DISGUSTING

Rita Arens SURRENDER, DOROTHY

Childhood constipation.

Yes, this is about constipation. You might want to just stop reading now. It's not going to be for the faint of heart.

The little angel's favorite foods are, in order: mac and cheese, milk, yogurt, and bananas. See a pattern here? She also eats a lot of fiber, but it seems that her favorite foods are interfering with her digestive tract.

It just started a few months ago. She would cry and stare pathetically off into the distance as she grunt, grunt, grunted. Then she would look at me with bucket-sized tears streaming down her face and utter one word: "Poopy."

My best friend's mother once told me (when she witnessed one of these spells) that I should *help* her. At the time, I was all, "No way am I doing that. *No way.*" Then about two weeks ago, I had to do it. She was so uncomfortable. She was doing everything right, and alas, it was just not working. I laid her down on the changing table to check for progress.

I saw it crown.

I thought *No. There is no way that I am doing it.*

Then, you know, I did. I helped. I covered my hands with plastic bags. It was sort of like pulling baseball-sized modeling clay out of an eel. It was the most disgusting and loving thing I have ever done in my entire life. I was so grossed out that only watching my best friend pick up a decomposed mouse when I was three months pregnant and very sick beats it out for Most Disgusting Event Ever. But I did it, because I. Am. Her. Mother.

THE DINNER PARTY

Joanna Polyn THE MODERNITY WARD

Imagine that you, the child, have gathered all your dearest friends, spiritual leaders, beloved family members, and workplace superiors at your home for a dinner event. A lavish meal is set out, and you yourself partake heartily of the fare, which includes many fresh figs from the trees outside. Everyone has a wonderful time talking, laughing, and enjoying the dinner, with you as the center of attention, the exalted hostess, a one-year-old sun that shines over the party.

Now imagine that the dishes are being cleared in preparation for dessert. You pay a quick visit to the bathroom and return to stand next to your chair.

"Ladies, gentlemen, wise advisors, and respected elders, I have brought you here today," you begin, "to thank you for—"

A strange look passes over your face. Your mother, seated across the table from where you totter on your pudgy feet, recognizes it. "Oh, she's pooping," she informs the room.

And indeed you are, as soon becomes obvious to all the attendees, since you have neglected to replace your pants after your most recent bathroom visit. This is all your mother's fault, dammit. She said you'd tee-teed, and could therefore have nakey bottom time! But there's no time to think because, oh God, you're pooping some more!

The partygoers scramble to assist you in your hour of embarrassment. "Get the potty," says your father. "Wow, that's a really long turd!" "It is, isn't it? What a loooooong turd! Yes!" Your grandmother says cheerily. No one seems upset by this turn of events. This is not the flourish you'd envisioned to end your party. You begin to weep.

Your father removes you gently from the scene, and while he is holding you, awaiting delivery of wet wipes, you feel that certain stirring in your bowels again. The humiliation! You begin to wail at the injustice, to struggle indignantly.

"Oh! More poo-poo!" Your mother is trying to put on a happy face. "Oh, dear God, it's, I mean, oh my! Why, it seems to be getting on the carpet! Mama had better find herself a scrub brush! Well, well, well."

Meanwhile, Dada holds you over the potty in the kitchen, trying to catch what is now dangling from your buttocks. You hate him for drawing more attention to your plight, so you kick at the potty, which at this point has received its unspeakable cargo. Now you've got poo-poo on your foot.

"Poo-poo on your foot!" Dada says, brightly. "Let's go to the bathroom! Maybe you could sit on the big potty! That's fun, right?" His attempts to soothe you are all for naught, and you continue to scream as Mama applies hot, soapy water to the rug before somebody steps in it, please.

"Uh, I need some help in here," calls Dada, over your shrieks. He sounds a little desperate, and who could blame him? You've nearly squirmed yourself into the toilet, and he's now trying to sit you on the little potty in the bathroom long enough to wipe the worst of it off your legs. You are inconsolable. You are also pooping again.

Mama arrives, shirt hiked up, and nurses you right there on the potty while Dada wipes. And oh, blessed nursing! Calm returns. You regain your composure. Breathe deeply. Poop a little more. And finally, finally, you look up at Mama and Dada, smiling.

Eventually, wiped and soaped and rinsed and diapered, you return to the table, ready once again to preside. Your guests marvel at the length of your poops, the sheer volume, you see, when taken in aggregate. Perhaps it was all the figs, they say. Why, that must have been the entire contents of your large intestine! You nod, pleased, and grab another fig, thinking: we really must do this again sometime.

VISITING MY HOUSE?
BRING YOUR OWN AUTOCLAVE
Sheryl Naimark PAPER NAPKIN

A few weeks ago, Haley began to wet the bed. She wears Pull-Ups, mind you, which hold approximately eight gallons of fluid, but apparently my four-year-old has a bladder the size of the tanks at SeaWorld, and her Pull-Ups often overflow. After she soaks her sheets and strips off her sopping pajamas, she stumbles sleepily into our bed and falls asleep. Near morning, as we're all slumbering peacefully in our nest of snuggles, SHE PEES ON US.

Y'all, may I just say, I am tired of the pee. *Tired. Of. The. Pee.* Also, the laundry. We are a family of five, generating enough laundry for a family of twelve coal miners. I've trained *dogs* who didn't pee this much, and if I didn't know better I'd swear she was marking her territory. Maybe one afternoon, if she and her brother are fighting over the toy du jour, she could just snatch it away, drop her pants, and take a whiz on it. Not that her brother isn't guilty of wildly wielding the golden hose once in a while. Between the two of them I'd like to flush the whole house.

Googling for bed-wetting solutions, I found an electronic alarm that you affix in your child's pajamas. When it senses moisture, it sounds an ear-piercing alarm. People really buy this? Maybe people with one child. I can just see our house when the alarm sounds: Aaron and I jump out of bed and race around like the Keystone

Cops, Emily calls 911, Will wakes up crying and doesn't go back to sleep until dawn, and Haley sleeps through the alarm and is floating in Pee Lake. But hey! At least I can be sleep deprived while I do the laundry!

If not for the risk of electrocution, I think a sensor that gives a kid a little shock is a better idea—no sleep loss for the parents. Although there could be sterilization issues if you're continually zapping your son in the badoobies, I suppose, so you'd have to weigh the pros and cons. Hmm, more sleep or no grandchildren, that's a toughie.

According to one Web site I perused, in Africa, a live frog is strapped to the child as a "natural" alarm. Ah, yes, nothing makes me feel quite as close to nature as having a frog between my legs. A close second to wearing my hedgehog epaulets with my raccoon bustier. It's the next best thing to camping in Yosemite.

I can just picture it. You Velcro the frog in your child's undies and play *The Sounds of Croaking* to lull them both to sleep. She's blissfully unaware there's an amphibian in her pants until 2:00 A.M., when the screaming ensues.

Or, your child is so excited at the prospect of a pet that she requests to bring it to school, for Show and Tell. "This is Milo. He keeps me dry at night."

Or, you hear a small voice in the middle of the night. "Mama can you bring me a glass of water? And bring a live cricket for Milo. He wants a snack."

Don't get me wrong, I think pets are an important part of childhood. But for now I think I'll just make her sleep naked in the bathtub.

4

Never Enough Time for Everything

It doesn't matter if you work outside the home or parent full-time: no parent retains more than one serious hobby or set of friends during those first energy-draining few years. Children sense our yearning for freedom. They know they are the gatekeepers and the keymasters. And they like it.

THE STARBUCKS AT THE END OF THE UNIVERSE

Amy Corbett Storch AMALAH

So let's say you have plans to meet someone at a nearby Starbucks at 3:45 on an average Thursday afternoon. Let's also say that you are pretty much a total shut-in these days and the whole endeavor is pretty much the social event of your week.

(We don't even need to say how pathetically sad you are, because honestly, YOU ARE PATHETICALLY SAD.)

2:00 Hey, you know what? I should totally leave now. I'd be all early and relaxed and delicately sipping a nonfat latte, that I totally won't spill on the baby, when my friend arrives instead of flying in all harebrained, disheveled, and late like I usually do.

2:03 I could take my impossibly tiny new laptop with me and write a blog entry! Or maybe even a book!

2:04 Oh my God, *totally*. I could get at least one, maybe two whole chapters written! I will sit in the plushy chairs by the fireplace and maybe get part of the proposal done, too.

2:06 Also should find an agent. Can you find agents on Google?

2:10 Should probably give Noah a bottle first.

2:20 Please don't spit up on me, please don't spit up on . . .

2:21 Damn it.

2:23 OK! New shirt! Pretty pink boho shirt! Matches fabulous pink Prada sandals!

2:25 Dilemma. Pants too long for pink Prada sandals. Pants make ass look not huge.

2:26 Kicky espadrille wedges it is!

2:28 Did I shower today? I did shower today. Or am I thinking of yesterday?

2:29 Sniff.

2:30 Well, I definitely forgot deodorant this morning, THAT MUCH IS CERTAIN.

2:33 Hair up? Hair down? Hair up?

2:37 Up. Definitely up. Makeup would be nice too.

2:53 Let's change the baby's diaper.

2:54 Poop! Of course. OF COURSE.

2:59 SOMETIMES IN LIFE WE JUST HAVE TO WEAR CLOTHING, NOAH, AND THIS IS ONE OF THOSE TIMES.

3:05 ALSO I CAN YELL LOUDER THAN YOU, AHHHHHHHHHHHHHHH.

3:10 Who the *fuck* took all the diapers out of the diaper bag? *Who?* Oh, right, the pooping.

3:13 Shove diapers, burp cloths, bibs, extra outfit, plastic keys ($1.69 replacement keys for exact same 99-cent keys the dog ate, like, fucking inflation, man), and plastic measuring cup in bag.

3:15 Walk past mirror. Hair down. Down!

3:16 If I leave right this instant, I will have fifteen minutes to spare. I could at least get most of a blog entry done, plus maybe the acknowledgments for a book.

3:17 Hmmm. Sky looks vaguely ominous.

3:18 Will pack that stroller rain cover thing we've never used, just in case.

3:20 Should I bring umbrella? Logistics of pushing stroller and negotiating umbrella seem daunting. Will grab Coach rain hat instead.

3:22 OUT THE FRONT DOOR, OH MY GOD.

3:24 Stroller is in car. Hmmm. What to do with the baby while I unload the stroller from the trunk? Access to car seat is blocked by boxes of baby clothes I totally meant to mail to my sister, like, three months ago, and also office desk lamps.

3:25 After a moment of deliberation, decide to stick Noah in driver's seat and buckle the seatbelt around his waist, and, holy fuck, I am very glad the whole "Internet Rockstar" thing is total petty bullshit, because the paparazzi would be all over my ass for this.

3:29 Stroller is bulky and heavy and arrrgh, it's starting to drizzle. Seriously, if I'm such a fucking rockstar WHERE IS MY PERSONAL ASSISTANT, BITCHES?

3:30 ALSO, GROUPIES AND BLOW. I DON'T HAVE THOSE, EITHER.

3:32 Pry Noah's jaws off steering wheel, put Noah in stroller, realize you can totally see down my shirt when I bend over.

3:33 Shit. It's totally pouring now.

3:34 Stroller cover! Am world's best mother and trip-to-Starbucks planner.

3:36 How the hell?

3:38 What the fuck?

3:39 ARRRGGH, SUBMIT YOU PLASTIC MONSTER. SUBMIT!

3:40 Huh. That's pretty damn cool. Except, can he *breathe* in there? It's like I've just put a plastic grocery bag over his head.

3:41 Put on hat, jacket, start walking confidently down Wisconsin Avenue like the rain isn't bothering me at *all* and I can totally powerwalk ten blocks in four minutes, are you kidding me?

3:42 Ugh, my hands are already pruny.

3:44 Oh my God. It's the fucking apocalypse.

3:45 A woman, in her mad desire to get around me (I gave up powerwalking about two minutes ago), nails me in the head with her umbrella. Sidewalk rage!

3:45.23 OMG IF U WERE 3 FEET SHORTER U WOULD HAV HIT MY PRESHUS BABIE!

3:46 Stroller cover is impenetrable shield, deflecting all raindrops directly onto me.

3:47 Pink shirt, when wet, has taken on the unfortunate shape of a maternity top.

3:48 Noah and his Impenetrable Shield are very amusing to people, apparently.

3:49 Glance down, realize bra is showing.

3:49.17 Oh God, am one bottle-fed infant away from being Katie Holmes.

3:50 Sun! The sun! Yet it rains on.

3:51 Pants are so wet that my laptop would probably electrocute me.

3:52 *Sun.* No more rain. At all! In fact . . .

3:53 SUUUUN. HOT. DYING. HATE.

3:54 Decide to stop and take off jacket and hat, perhaps is time to check that Noah is, like, alive and stuff.

3:55 He's asleep, all flopped-over-ragdoll-Sean-Preston-like. Decide to poke him, just in case.

3:55.12 He moved! Well, that's a plus.

3:56 Walk past Metro stop where forty plillion high school students are congregating. Dread fear of roving groups of teenagers second only to volcanoes.

3:57 Catch reflection in store window. Put hat back on. Wow.

3:57:45 DO NOT LOOK TEENAGERS DIRECTLY IN THE EYES. IT CHALLENGES THEM.

3:59 At next walk signal, feel slight tap on arm, turn to see teenage girl. I am going to die now. Girl asks where Metro stop is. I point. She smiles sweetly and says thank you. God, they are so good at pretending to be normal sometimes.

4:01 Am muttering to Noah about disowning him if he ever dares enter puberty while I struggle with door to Starbucks.

4:02 Say hi to Stacy as I fly in, all harebrained, disheveled, and, surprise, late.

5:00 Leave to go home. Do not dare attempt to write at Starbucks, as it was fucking crawling with teenagers who would probably beat me to death with my laptop or at least make fun of my stupid hat.

UNDER "OCCUPATION,"
I USUALLY WRITE "DILETTANTE"

Susan Wagner FRIDAY PLAYDATE

Wade comes home from work at night, and after we talk about his day and the kids' days, he says, "How was your day?"

And I say, "Eh. Fine." And then I struggle to think about what exactly I did all day. Usually I come up with really thrilling things, like *I balanced the checkbook* or *I went to the grocery* or *I spent an hour on hold with the insurance company.*

It's a wild life, mine is.

For six years, I've had a child with me almost constantly; before that, I worked, more or less full-time. Because I was an academic, a large part of my "work" was reading and writing and thinking about things. I loved that, and I miss it. I've always had something to do, something more than just cooking and keeping my house clean, and I never really minded the housewife things because they weren't my job.

I used to think about how great it would be just to have time—no deadlines or office hours or feeding schedules. Now I have time, and I don't know what the hell to do with it.

I take the boys to school at eight and I pick them up at three. In between, I clean up the house, start laundry, load and unload the dishwasher, think about dinner, pay bills, fill out forms, and make appointments. On Wednesdays, I have coffee with Christa. I read some, and I write some. And then the day is over and I don't really know what I've done.

This morning, at our coffee date, Christa was talking about wanting to work less, to be home more with her children in this last year before they are both in school full-time. That's funny, I said, because I want to work more. We talked about how our mothers both played tennis when we were kids, how that was part of what you did when you were the stay-at-home mom. "You could play tennis," Christa said.

"Maybe," I told her. "But, honestly? I would feel guilty about playing tennis while Wade was working a fifteen-hour day."

"Yes," she said.

I'm not ready to go back to work in any traditional sense; my family isn't ready for me not to be here at home taking care of things. Twice in the last week I have left the house without my cell phone, and when I realized that I had been out of touch, I panicked. What if someone was hurt? Or sick? My job is to be there.

No one was hurt. Or sick. And I'm always here, more or less.

For literally years, Wade has been saying, "You should go on vacation! Go to Minneapolis and see Cheryl! Go see your parents! Go see your brother! Leave the kids with me!" He has always been serious and sincere, and I've always agreed that yes, I should go, and yes, I will go, but I've never gone. When my friends and I started planning our trip to Kansas City, Wade said, "Go! I'll take two days off work! It's fine!"

He can't take two days off work; he's busier now than he ever has been. And it is fine, and he will do fine with the boys, but as I race around today trying to get everything ready for him (making lunches and writing out phone numbers and drawing little maps of the schools so he knows where to find the boys when he goes to get them, and charging my cell phone just in case someone calls me first), I am shocked by the amount of stuff I do around here.

My job seems to be to know things, like where the aftercare room is and who takes which medications and how many pairs of pants each boy has. I need to remember to leave Wade a note about milk money for Charlie. I need to be sure to have him check each boy's folder after school for homework. I need to be sure all three of them have clean underwear.

This is what I do all day, and while it doesn't take seven hours, someone has to do it. I am incredibly grateful that we are able to have me do this, all the time, without worrying about how we will pay the bills. I know that for my family—*my family*, not necessarily anyone else's—this is the best choice. But recently I've been thinking that I want something else to do, something that will challenge my mind and give me something to talk about at the end of the day, something more than shopping for shoes or playing tennis. I'm looking right now for some small kind of work, because even though I know that I do a tremendous amount here, even though I know that what I do is valuable and valued, I need something more.

"If you wish at once to do nothing and be respectable nowadays," Leslie Stephen wrote in 1865, "the best practice is to be at work on some profound study." I think I'm searching for the profound study that will give me some respectability while I do nothing all day. But first, I have to move some laundry and dig up some milk money for Charlie.

WHO'S NOT A WORKING PARENT?

Rita Arens SURRENDER, DOROTHY

The debates of parenthood, how they rage. And they take so many prisoners.

To work outside the home or not is one of the most hotly contested debates in the mommy continuum. I struggled mightily with this one. I fancied myself having a choice. There are many ardent stay-at-home mommies out there who would probably maintain that I did have a choice, even if my choice meant selling This Old House, for which I paid (are you listening, coastal dwellers?) a whopping $127,500. We would've had to move to a two-bedroom apartment and sell a car to stay afloat on my beloved's salary, and to do that very well might have meant sacrificing matrimonial harmony. I chose my marriage, not wanting to face the arguments that can come from eating noodles with butter three hundred times in a row. I kept working.

My working-mommy mentor told me that it took her a good six months to feel comfortable working outside the home after going back from maternity leave. It took me longer than that—almost a year—before the little angel came up on the waiting list at the Emerald City and started skipping off to daycare most days. There are days that she clings to my leg and cries, and those are the days when I must explain to her that we all have our jobs, and mine is to go to work and earn money, Daddy's is to go to work and do whatever he does there (I kid my husband), and hers is to go to school and play with her posse and maybe make Mommy and Daddy a nice picture out of those noodles we won't be eating more than twice a week because I stayed employed.

My friend Maureen recently went back to work after having her baby. She's currently immersed in the crying jags that come from leaving your precious child after spending every moment with him or her for three months. I remember it well. I remember questioning myself as a human being. I watched my friend Ann make her own decision to cut back to part-time, and she can do that, because she can afford to do that. I applaud her. My friend Cindy in Chicago does the same. I envy them their extra child time, but I also have realized after a lot of soul searching that we have to live the life in front of us, as my best friend once told me. And you do.

I've missed out on some things the little angel has done that I would've liked to have seen. I've also missed out on her doing some other things that I'm glad I didn't see. There are trade-offs either way. I miss out every workday on watching her make her pictures or go down her slides or dance with scarves, but I also miss out on her being cranky and getting time-outs, if she gets them. I'll never know. This may sound incredibly callous, but I do know that from the minute I see her after work until the minute I go to bed and every minute of every weekend, I enjoy her. Part of this can be attributed to her genial personality, but part of it is that I come to the table reasonably fresh. I also have a cleaning lady who comes twice a month and a job that provides me with the lovely feedback every adult needs.

I don't see many working mothers owning their positions. There's a lot of guilt out there, a cultural belief that despite the fact that 68 percent of mothers work outside the home, we're doing it wrong. We should be at home, raising our kids. To that, I have to say that I *am* raising my daughter. And so are some very lovely individuals at her school and a cadre of sticky-fingered four-year-olds who are teaching my only child that she is not the only human being on the planet, that she sometimes has to share and wait in line and that if someone pulls the fire alarm she should grab the string with the rings on it and get the hell out of Compton. Those women love my daughter, and we love them.

The little angel's lead daycare teacher's husband died when my daughter was two. It was the first experience the little angel had with mourning. We learned that people are sometimes sad, and when they are, we should give them extra hugs and be very nice to them. She had a little girl in her class who has cystic fibrosis, and so she's learned not to fear wheelchairs or special equipment, and that Cecilia can still play even if play means having the other kids bring over their toys or books and share their lives with her. It's much easier for me to explain disabilities now—I can just say that the ramp is what Cecelia needs to move her chair, or that person over there? He is like Cecilia, and he just needs people to involve him in their lives. These are valuable lessons.

When I had the little angel, I was extremely overprotective. I still totally am. Many people told me what I needed was to have another child. What they really meant is that I needed to cede control. Daycare has made me do that—I can't control every morsel that goes in her mouth or every experience to which she is exposed. She learns songs I don't even know, and I have to ask her to teach them to me. She just laughs and says, "Silly Mommy." How many things will she learn that I will never know?

Childcare is hard. There are no nonworking parents. I have several friends who are stay-at-home moms, and their lives are not necessarily easier than mine, but they're not necessarily harder, either. They're just *different*. Knowing that we will probably not have another child, I am thankful the little angel has found peers in her little posse. I'm thankful she has somewhere to go every weekday and feels safe in a place other than our home. I'm thankful she's met people of all races at a very early age and will not grow to fear people who look different. I'm not saying no stay-at-home mom could expose their child to that environment, but I don't know how easily I would've done it if I were alone with her. I live in the Midwest. I have friends of other races, but I don't have a plethora of them with four-year-old kids.

Most of all, though, the past four years have taught me that there are not as many choices in parenting as you think there are. Children are little people, and they have their own little personalities. We don't control their sleeping, eating, and pooping as much as we'd like to think we do. We don't control the price of gas or the war in Iraq. We don't control downsizing or upsizing, and we barely control our mortgages with the rising interest rates. We just do the best we can. We live the lives in front of us.

The one thing we can control is how we treat each other. How much we judge each other. Each time I'm envious of one of my stay-at-home mommy friends, I remind myself that I get props at work, I get to have lunch with other adults, and I get to not be covered in goo for about eight hours a day. I get to sneak off to the gym at lunchtime and have a ten-minute drive to myself, during which I may run a child-free errand. And I have that moment that stay-at-home mommies don't get—the moment my little angel looks up at daycare, realizes I've walked in the door, and runs to me screaming with joy. Then she drags me over to a table to show me the dinosaur she's just slaughtered for dinner.

I hope that she'll remember these times and not be upset that I wasn't there all the time. I also hope that I'll be one of the lucky ones who gets to work part-time when she is school-aged, so that I can be there for her when she gets off the big, yellow bus. I hope that will happen, but if it doesn't, I'll still focus on her when I get home and listen to every detail of her day and make her feel like the most important person in the world when we are together. Because other than my beloved, she is the most important person in the world to me. Because of that, we deal with our situation, and we try to make lemonade, even if it occasionally spills.

STATE OF GRACE
Jenny Lauck THREE KID CIRCUS

I've been manic the last couple of days—and my kids are starting to lose patience with my sorry self. I've told them, "No. Not now. Mommy's busy. I can't. I don't. Later. Wait."

I know I've been expecting a lot and giving the bare minimum. I have a lot of catch-up work to do, and while I sit in front of the computer trying to deliver some of the work I've promised to other people, my children have been repeatedly pushed away. Chubby hands reach for the mouse in frustration, and I have found myself snarling at the owner of those delicious dimples, "Don't touch."

My youngest is going through a big identifying phase. Everything gets a label, and she usually prefaces the label with "my." My shoes. My toy. My house.

She managed to clamber up into my lap while I tried in vain to continue typing. She sucked her thumb and rested her cheek against my chest as I tried to work around her. After a minute or two of that, I began to gather her up into my arms so that I could once again find another place to put her, away from my working zone.

She grabbed both my ears in her tiny talons and put her nose to my nose and said, "My. Mommy." I couldn't help it. I just started to cry. I don't know how work-at-home parents do it. I settled myself on the couch with my baby clinging to me with a ferociousness that let me know I've put her down and walked away one too many times in the last couple of days.

We sat there, just leaning on each other, breathing in tandem. My son approached, and quietly sat next to me and pulled my arm around his shoulders. He melted into my side, and we just sat quietly together. Both kids gave me gentle, almost subconscious kisses on my arms, my shoulders, whatever they could reach. It was a benediction, full of the promise of forgiveness for the lack of care I sometimes take with the precious gifts I have been given.

HAPPY FREAKIN' NEW YEAR
Risa Green MOMMY TRACK'D

I put a lot of thought into my New Year's resolutions. I don't do lame ones that are destined to fail, like eat less sugar or clean out my closet. Instead, I try to find some behavior that is bringing me down somehow, and I resolve to change it. This year I've got a doozy. My resolution for this year is to pretend that I am twenty years older and that I have been given a chance to go back in time and relive this period of my life. It's a mouthful, I know. Eat less sugar would have been so much simpler. Obviously, I'm not doing so well with my previous New Year's resolution, which was to try to not make things more complicated than they need to be.

But really, I think I'm on to something with this one. In twenty years, I'll be fifty-five. My kids will be twenty-two and twenty-four. My husband will be fifty-four. If fifty-five-year-old me could go back and be thirty-five-year-old me again, I think that fifty-five-year-old me would A) be really psyched to not have so many wrinkles, and B) do some things a little differently.

For example, my son is two years old. He whines a lot and he's going through a super-clingy phase. He always wants me to pick him up, he'll only let me put him to bed, and I can't escape his room without a minimum of forty hugs before he'll lie down in his crib. Now, this stuff drives me insane, especially when I'm starving and want to eat dinner and he's yelling for me to come back into his room to give him his forty-seventh hug, or when I'm trying to talk on the phone to my editor and he's crying and screaming, "Uppy, Mommy, uppy," at the top of his lungs.

But then I think about fifty-five-year-old me. Fifty-five-year-old me would probably kill for the chance to pick up her son (who, let's not forget, is now twenty-two), and have him wrap his arms around her neck and squeeze her so hard that she very nearly loses consciousness. Hell, with the way my back feels these days, fifty-five-year-old me would probably just be thrilled to not be an invalid anymore. And you see, when you think about it that way, you can't help but be less annoyed by the kid, and more appreciative of just how sweet it is to have a little person love you so much that he just wants to be close to your face, even if it is at a particularly inconvenient time.

It works with other stuff, too. Sex, for example. When I think about fifty-five-year-old me, all menopausal and hot-flashy and saggy, not to mention her fifty-four-year-old husband (ahem) it makes me want to muster up the energy more often. Fifty-five-year-old me must long for the days when the only barrier to sex was being too tired.

It works with my mother—she might be crazy now, but God only knows what she'll be like in twenty years, if she's even here at all. It even works with work. When I'm stressed out over a deadline, or late for a meeting because my daughter insisted on buttoning her sweater all by herself, I conjure fifty-five-year-old me, and she tells me to relax. "One day," she whispers, "when you're an empty nester and your life is predictable, quiet, and completely your own, you'll miss this chaos. You'll miss it terribly."

I look at her, my eyebrow cocked with skepticism, and I ask her if she really means that. But she just smiles back, with her wrinkles and her grey hair colored blonde. "Absolutely," she answers. "Now have a happy freakin' New Year, drink some champagne, and go have sex with your hot husband, because he's not gonna look like this forever. And for God's sake, don't forget to wear sunscreen. Collagen doesn't grow on trees, you know."

SO, WHAT DO YOU DO?

Kelli Oliver George RANCID RAVES

A year ago, I would have said, "I work for the Federal Reserve doing data security." Now I reply, "I stay home full-time with my son."

Last Friday marked a full year of what I like to refer to as "this staying gig." I can't put my finger on why, but it still makes me chuckle when I say I stay at home. Why "stay"? It suggests the image of me merely sitting on my couch all day twiddling my thumbs, not "going," just "staying."

But I digress. I have to confess that it has been twelve blissful months, and in particular, I'd like to give a shout-out to my husband. Last year, I was all set to work up to a few weeks before my due date, but the Fed was getting pretty miserable after a painful reorganization. My new boss was passive-aggressive and would berate me for leaving a meeting when I needed to puke, or she would pull bullshit like berating me for not having sent her a file (when I would point out that I did send the file, she would proceed to berate me for not naming it something that she would easily recognize). In short, there was much berating. Bitter much? Nah, not me.

Anyway, my husband was the one to push me to quit more than three months before Arun's due date, and I was all "Don't Cry for Me, Argentina" as my fat pregnant ass waddled out the door past the metal detectors. Hands down, those last three months of my pregnancy were some of the happiest months of my life.

I was able to relish being pregnant and just take it easy. Whenever Arun would start kicking, which was often, I would just stop and enjoy the moment. I am forever grateful that I had those months to pamper myself and was able to get the house in order before Arun arrived.

Then Arun did arrive, and the next few months were some of the hardest in my life. None of the baby books prepared me for a baby that wanted to be held all the time. A fussy, high-maintenance bundle of boy who was all "me, me, *me*."

Did I mention that he wanted to be held *all the fucking time*? Before Arun, I was all, "Co-sleepers are granola-grained *fuh-reaks*," until the universe totally bitch-slapped me, and I had a baby who slept like rock with me and only with me. But we adjusted, came to mutual terms, and life is good now. It was the hand I was dealt, and I played it as best I could. But as hard it was, I never felt I was making some huge monumental sacrifice, and I am well aware that not punching the snooze button at 6:00 A.M. has something to do with it. Believe it or not, I have tried really hard not to complain too much, because I appreciate the perk of sleeping in late or catching a nap.

I've always known that I would want to stay home full-time, if possible. I've always known that with my slightly obsessive personality I would've felt torn between being a yes-woman in the office and a yes-Mama at home, without getting either quite right.

I am glad that I had the years to be able to focus on my career—I've worked a lot of hours and traveled a lot of miles. I have no regrets. It made it all that easier to give it up for now. Besides, my career was just one part of me, and while Arun has come in to take its place for the time being, the other parts of me are still there—although some are dormant (God, I miss raku).

THIS WEEK IN GUILT
Amy Corbett Storch AMALAH

So, week two. My first almost-full week with Noah in daycare, minus Monday, which means next week could suck progressively more.

I hate it. I hate it, hate it, hate it.

Noah loves it.

So there you go.

Tuesday

I have a conversation with a mother in Noah's room about the fabulousity of the Dr. Brown's bottles as we carefully label our children's food with colored tape and a Sharpie.

The other mother is labeling a dizzying array of bottles, fruit, and cereal for her nine-month-old and casually mentions that she never tried the wide-necked Dr. Brown's because her daughter was never breastfed. I look down at my standard, non-wide-necked bottles and quietly mumble that Noah is breastfed but still never liked the wide-necks, and then realize that I sound like a total asshole.

I write *breastmilk* on two of Noah's bottles—bottles that required four days' worth of pumping to fill—and I write *formula* on the last one and shove it in the back of the fridge. Asshole.

As I leave, I see Noah's eyes widen as he scans the room, looking for me. I make a choked-up, gasping noise that startles a staff member walking by, and she asks me if I'm OK. I affirm that I am and quickly walk away. I make it all the way back to the car before I start crying.

Every working mother at work stops by to offer encouragement and promises that it will get easier.

When I go back at noon to nurse him, he's settled in and barely notices that it's me, Mama, *the one they cut you out of and who still cannot poop right because of it,* until my shirt is open and hello! Boobs! But he keeps pulling away because he wants to turn around and see what the other babies are doing. He's fascinated by them, particularly the two older babies who can sit up and crawl. One of the teachers notices him watching the room and sings out his name, and he squeals with delight.

They play music to the infants all day long, lullabies and sing-along songs and classical music. I realize how many *Simpsons* episodes have probably already embedded themselves in Noah's subconscious and feel a twinge of guilt.

When I pick him up in the evening, his teachers have written notes on his schedule to tell me how much they love him already. Jason isn't nearly as touched as I am, because "You know they're probably told to do that for the all new parents. So you won't freak out and withdraw in a week and not give them all your money."

Yeah, I know. But I quietly paste the schedule into Noah's baby book when Jason isn't looking.

Wednesday

I notice that there are a lot of dads who do the morning drop-off. They look only slightly less pained than the mothers.

There's a notice posted that the center has a confirmed case of the chicken pox.

I've never had the chicken pox but can't get vaccinated until I stop breastfeeding. I put three bottles of formula in the fridge, because I only managed to pump two measly ounces the day before.

Today, Noah doesn't look for me. He's all smiles and baby talk as I slip out of the room.

I'm really tired.

An older woman at work welcomes me back and asks to see photos of Noah. She asks me about childcare, and I only get as far as, "He's at a daycare center right down the—" before she scrunches up her face and makes a sad little "Oh!" sound.

When I drive over at lunch, there's a woman panhandling at an intersection. She's holding a sign that reads HOMELESS MOTHER OF THREE CHILDREN PLEASE HELP GOD BLESS YOU. I'm sure it's a scam—other days there's a guy here with a different sign who claims to be a Vietnam veteran—so I keep my window up and my eyes straight ahead. I feel really shitty by the time the light turns green.

His teachers are feeding two babies their cereal when I arrive. I quietly nurse him in the corner and try to ignore the baby who is howling in his crib to be picked up. The teachers call to him and sing and hurriedly feed the older ones before they go get him.

Part of me is horrified at the thought of Noah being left to cry all those agonizing minutes, and part of me remembers how that very morning I let him cry while I packed up his bottles and extra clothes while Jason hurriedly walked the dog. And then how he cried again when I put him down while I looked for my keys in the couch cushions.

At home that evening, Noah cries. A lot. I worry he's getting sick until I, going on sleep-deprived autopilot, call him Handsome Boy. It's his teacher's nickname for him. He immediately smiles and laughs.

Huh.

Thursday

This is easy! Dropping him off is great! Look how happy he is! God. Why is he so happy? Why doesn't he scream like he does at home? Why did he cry all night last night and refuse to nurse? Why won't he stop smiling at his teacher? Why does he like these women better than me?

The center announces that it also has a confirmed case of pink eye.

I'm really, really tired.

Noah nurses distractedly at lunch again, and I'm getting the distinct feeling that the lunchtime visits are definitely more for my benefit than his. The more bottles he takes, the less patience he has for breastfeeding, and what's worse, the chubbier he gets.

I always assumed Noah was just one of those long, skinny babies. One week in daycare and big, fat bottles of formula, and he's getting a double chin and fat rolls on his thighs.

"My *God*," I tell Jason on the phone, my voice quivering, "I've been *starving* him for TWELVE WEEKS. What kind of STUPID PERSON am I?"

Jason says it's probably just a growth spurt, but my hatred of my stupid, nonproducing boobs burns once again.

When I arrive to take Noah home, one teacher has gone home and an aide is helping out until the room gets down to three babies. (Maryland law states that the ratio must be one teacher for every three infants.) She has Noah on a Boppy pillow and is singing to him. He's transfixed and smiling.

I pick him up and realize his diaper leaked and his clothes are wet.

His teacher is horrified. She chastises the aide for not noticing. She assures me that she just changed him less than a half hour before. She pulls out his chart to show me, that yes, he had been changed recently. She snaps at the aide again.

I suddenly realize she thinks I'm angry.

I laugh and assure her that this is Noah's favorite trick, and that I can't count the number of times I changed him, only to replace his entire outfit (or better still, his outfit *and* mine) fifteen minutes later. Diapers leak, and my boy pees a lot.

She doesn't seem convinced and apologizes again. Then tells me that Noah drank all the bottles I brought that morning and was acting hungry and fussy, but they didn't have anything for him. Could I bring in an extra bottle tomorrow in case it happens again?

And now it's my turn to be horrified. I apologize. I stammer. I go on and on about how I don't know how many bottles he needs since I nurse him at home. I tell them about the can of powdered formula in his cubby, but learn that the center meant a can of the *premixed* formula, because of the rules about using tap water in the babies' bottles or something, and oh my God, I DIDN'T SEND IN ENOUGH FOOD FOR MY BABY. WHAT KIND OF MOTHER DOES THAT?

So we stand there for awhile, each frantically trying to explain a situation that didn't really need explaining, when Noah suddenly pees again. It arches up and in between us, and we both yelp and jump out of the way.

And he laughs, and we laugh, because we both just want the very best for this hilarious little person.

When I get home, I realize that we conceived Noah exactly one year ago tonight. Holy shit. When I remind Jason of this, we spend a few moments in awed silence, gazing at Noah and thinking about the million other ways our story could have ended, and how ridiculously, insanely blessed we are.

Friday

Noah is asleep in his carseat when I arrive in the morning. His teacher unhooks him and gently lays him in his crib. I put bottles of formula in the fridge—more bottles than he could possibly drink in a day—and go over to say good-bye. He opens his eyes and gives me a lazy smile.

And I fucking lose it.

I stand over his crib and sob. His teacher is alarmed and tentatively puts an arm around me. She tells me that he is happy here, and that they take special care of him. That they do everything they can to give him a mother's love.

I don't know how to tell her that's not it at all, and I cry harder.

The homeless woman with three kids is back at the intersection today. I roll down my window and give her a dollar.

Then I remember the ten dollars I paid earlier for the massage program my company offers every Friday, and I feel like shit again.

Noah is asleep today at lunch. I wake him up anyway and push him to nurse. He eats a little, but decides he'd rather watch his teachers as they sit on the floor with the other babies and sing song after song. Reluctantly, I let him join the circle and creep out the door.

I'm so bone-tired I fall asleep within the first five minutes of my massage appointment. It's the best ten dollars I've ever spent.

I think my milk is drying up. I don't think Noah cares. The center has a confirmed case of strep throat. I use my shiny new office door lock and try in vain to pump a few ounces, staring at Noah's picture and suddenly creeping myself out by imagining a guy hunched over a photo of a naked woman with the same intense concentration for the task at hand.

It's not getting any easier.

I drove to the center tonight, exhausted and feeling just generally kind of weepy and shitty. I'm afraid of crying in front of his teachers again for some reason. I'm just so tired.

When I arrive, the aide tonight is a young girl with Down's Syndrome. The teacher introduces her as an early-education student from the local community college who is here for training. I smile too broadly and speak too chirpily, clearly trying to communicate that I think this is great! I don't have a problem with this at all! I am not judging!

Asshole.

I pack Noah up, and she talks to him and tells me how many ounces of formula he drank and how many times she burped him. She's very sweet and well-spoken and coaxes smiles from Noah as I buckle him into his hated, hated carseat.

And now we're home. Hanging out, listening to a CD of lullabies and waiting for Daddy to get home.

I wish I had a nice happy ending for this post. I wish I could tell you that I feel blessed and fulfilled and am a better mother for using daycare and I was able to pump ten ounces at work today and blah blah blaaaaaaaaaaah. I'm too tired for any epiphanies or insight or heart-tugging treacle.

Right now I'm home with my beautiful, charming, and happy little boy on my lap, and he's drooling on my arm and yanking on my hair. I think he just pooped.

I'm so very, very happy right now.

5

Mommies Don't Need Med School

There was a commercial on when I was a teenager that went on and on about "Dr. Mom." It showed a smiling mother holding a bottle of some cough syrup (positioned so the label clearly showed), knowing with just a look exactly what was wrong with her child and which medicine (and the exact dosage) would fix him up in a jiffy. I thought, "Yeah, of course," and went on eating my popcorn.

Fast-forward to age thirty, when I came down with a wicked case of bronchitis while on a business trip one thousand miles from home. I flew home barely able to sit in my seat, drove straight to a walk-in clinic, and got my first ever breathing treatment. Then I drove home to find my daughter had a temperature of 105. After calling the pediatrician, I sat on the floor with my baby girl, wearing a mask to keep my dry hacking from spraying her flushed little face, pumping her full of infant Motrin and sponging her steaming flesh with a luke-warm washcloth. I had no idea what to do for her. I knew her fever was really high, and that was bad. I also knew I was the sickest I'd ever been, but she didn't want anyone to hold her but me.

Over the course of four years, I've learned how to tell if she has a temperature just by feeling her forehead or looking at her cheeks, but it took a first year in daycare, twelve or thirteen really high fevers, several childhood diseases (all caught by me), and tubes in her ears before I felt confident I knew what to do in most kiddie health crises. I remember calling a pediatrician hotline when she was eighteen months old and really sick and telling the doctor who answered, "I'm a new mom."

He asked how old my daughter was, and when I told him he replied, "No you're not! You're a veteran." Dr. Mom, my ass.

A MIGHTY WEAN

Liz Gumbinner MOM-101

We sat in a circle under the fluorescent lights of the windowless classroom, twenty-six strangers. Each face revealed the same emotions—apprehension, nervous anticipation, panic—only in different proportions. The matronly instructor looked up from her notes.

"Let's go around the circle, and you'll each tell us your name, a little about yourself, and what your biggest worry is regarding childbirth." The answers were predictable.

"Labor."

"Tearing."

"Needing forceps."

"Needing a C-section."

"Labor and tearing."

"Labor and tearing and needing a C-section and the epidural needle and Pitocin and taking care of the baby, OH MY GOD HOW AM I GOING TO TAKE CARE OF THE BABY?"

I know what you're thinking, but that last answer, that wasn't me.

My only concern was breastfeeding.

Unlike many women, I never romanticized breastfeeding. I hadn't thought about it much at all. But when I did, it seemed less of a beautiful moment between mother and child and more like playing host to a parasitic Mini-Me. I spent many sleepless pregnant nights readjusting the five pillows between my knees and pondering the awesome responsibility of sustaining another being solely with my body. I knew it was the right thing to do, but it just seemed so complicated. Reading Dr. Sears (bad idea, very bad idea) would lead you to believe that breastfeeding requires a two-month emotional preparation period, a La Leche League membership, several pre- and post-partum classes, a certified lactation consultant booked six weeks in advance, and mastery of his patented forty-seven-point, easy-latch-on technique.

Could I do this?

But then Thalia was born, and the milk came in, and, by God, there I was with my amorphous hospital-issue nightgown pulled to one side and a six pound, fifteen ounce baby at the proverbial teat.

(Six pounds, twelve ounces.)

(Six pounds, ten ounces.)

(Six pounds, seven ounces.)

(OK, she's got it down now. Nothing to see here. Move along.)

As it turns out, the female body was made for breastfeeding. Who knew? Of course, I had a bumpy start requiring nipple shields like something out of a deleted strip club scene from *Logan's Run*. Also, there was a brief but unpleasant episode of engorgement involving some F-cup-sized cabbage leaves. In retrospect, the cabbage leaves were sexy in a weird, green-leafy-vegetable-fetish kind of way. Thank you, thank you, readers of *Big Vegan Jugs* for voting me centerfold of the year. I'd like to thank my mom. And tofu.

Two weeks into it, we were in the groove. My body was mixing up a bottomless lacto-cocktail, and Thalia was imbibing with gusto. To my surprise it wasn't bad at all. The convenience! The bonding! The convenience! I breastfed where and when it was called for—in Barnes & Noble, on the benches of the Brooklyn promenade overlooking the East River, in my sister-in-law's living room in front of her very uncomfortable father. The poor man hasn't been the same since. I should really send a fruit basket.

My pièce de résistance was a cluster-feeding spectacular among the hallowed burgundy booths of Balthazar, where the celebrities deign to consume towering raw bar platters and steak frites alongside mere mortals. Oh, it was a beautiful sight. I wore white. Thalia wore pink. The openmouthed Euro couple facing us wore black. *A little milk with those bluepoints, chère?*

We were having a grand old time that summer, Thalia and me and my enormous boobs. We all got together ten, twelve times a day, and it was as though nothing could break up our happy little foursome.

Then I went back to work.

Work means travel. Travel means pumping.

Hauling that mad-scientist Medela contraption around was the least of my concerns. (Although every time I attached the cups and cranked up the juice, I felt like screaming, "On my count! One, two, three, CLEAR.") What I could not handle was squatting in a cramped bathroom stall in the Orlando airport for forty minutes with a manual pump sadistically tweaking my nipples raw while the most horrific sounds and smells drifted my way from the adjacent commodes.

On the second business trip, I pumped in the same airport bathroom, only for half the time. On the third trip, I only pumped at night in my hotel room. On the fourth trip, I brought my pump but never took it out of my bag. On the fifth trip, I left it at home altogether.

I had been surprised at how much I liked breastfeeding. Six months later, I was surprised at how much I liked not breastfeeding.

I'm happy I weaned. Is it OK to say that in this age of breastfeeding militants? I'm saying it.

To all those well-intentioned people who assured me that breast-feeding would make those forty-five pounds slide right off like butter on a hot biscuit: I experienced no such thing. But now having ceased nursing, I'm finally back on track to stuffing my hips into my neglected pre-pregnancy clothes. I'm walking a little taller these days, holding my head a little higher. It's amazing how much self-confidence is gained from the realization that I am no longer in danger of knocking small children to the ground with my ass as I pass them on the sidewalk.

I forgot how wonderful it is to eat Pop-Tarts for dinner without worrying that I'm depriving my child of some essential nutrients. I forgot how liberating it is to pop an Advil or an Allegra without first consulting six Web sites. And boy, do I love that I can have a glass of wine (or two or six) and it doesn't have to be timed around anything beside my own desire for a glass of wine (or two or six).

Above all, I am so very happy that the stained, elephantine bras I sported for too many months are crumpled up beneath the rest of the maternity clothes in a plastic Duane Reade bag in the back of the closet.

The 36DDDs are dead, long live the 36DDDs.

Of course I miss the sweet, still moments alone with Thalia. I am grateful to have been bequeathed so much uninterrupted time during which I could just smell the top of her head or study the curve of her shoulders or hear her make her little newborn squeaky-toy sounds as she ate. But in its place, I know there will be other moments. There always are.

As for you, Dr. Sears, we need to have a little sit-down, just you and me. No weapons. This time.

TODDLERS ARE LESS FUN
WHEN THEY'RE SICK

Alice Bradley FINSLIPPY

The child is sick and has been crying, crying, crying, nonstop, for hours every day. He's in a constant state of crisis, always frantically needing something that is impossible to deliver, because apparently, feverish toddlers believe that their teary protests will rend the fabric of reality so that the very item they desire will come bounding toward them from some alternate universe. So, for instance, he wants a cracker BUT NOT THAT CRACKER! OH GOD, I CAN'T BELIEVE YOU JUST OFFERED ME THE ONE CRACKER I DO NOT WANT. DAMN YOU! THE INJUSTICE! I WILL CLUTCH AT YOUR ANKLES AND WEEP WHILE POINTING AT THE SHELVES AT SOME OTHER BOX THAT ISN'T CRACKERS, BUT SWEET CHRIST! STOP TELLING ME IT ISN'T CRACKERS! JUST GIVE ME THE CRACKERS THAT SHOULD BE IN THERE! I DON'T CARE HOW IT'S DONE—I DON'T WANT TO HEAR YOUR LOGIC! I WILL SCREAM LOUDER, SO YOU GET THE POINT! AAAAAAIGH! NOW DO YOU SEE?

I am completely, utterly drained. I keep thinking he's feeling better and then I'll try to, say, put his shoes on, and he'll rip off the happy mask and shriek: I CAN'T BELIEVE YOU'RE PUTTING SHOES ON ME AT A MOMENT LIKE THIS, THE PRECISE MOMENT WHEN THE LAST THING I NEEDED OR COULD HANDLE WAS SHOES! I DEMAND TO GO OUTSIDE TO THE GLASS-AND-POOP-FESTOONED STREET, BUT I WILL

NEVER WEAR THOSE FOOT COVERINGS! YOU CAN'T MAKE ME LIVE BY YOUR RULES! HERE IS MORE SCREAMING FOR YOU!

He's finally taking a nap, although, GOD, I DON'T WANT TO, WHY DID YOU PUT ME IN THE CRIB OF DOOM?

AREN'T DOCTORS SUPPOSED TO MAKE YOU FEEL BETTER?

Liz Gumbinner MOM-101

I had always envisioned the perfect pediatrician as a cross between Mary Poppins and Maria Von Trapp. Unfortunately, my insurance company had no doctor fitting that description in their narrow list of approved providers in my neighborhood. As such, my daughter's pediatrician is more like a combination of Dr. Evil and Mel Brooks doing a Yoda impression.

This doctor is the type who slept through the bedside-manner lecture in med school but aced Advanced Condescension. While an excellent diagnostician and the doctor you want in your corner if something bad goes down, he seems to have little patience for new moms. (Read: new moms and their silly questions.) When his kinder, gentler partner isn't available for an appointment, I reluctantly schedule with him instead. Each time I do, I find I'm talking myself into it, psyching myself up as if it weren't a routine pediatric visit at all, but a debut appearance singing "The Star Spangled Banner" at Yankee Stadium. A cappella. Naked.

This will be the time he realizes I'm smart! This will be the time I become his number one favorite patient.

"So, what are you feeding her?" the doctor asked as he typed in Thalia's stats, never turning away from the computer screen. This wasn't unusual. He rarely looked me in the eyes.

"Um."

I squirmed in the folding chair where I sat holding the baby, kicking at the legs like an anxious fourth-grader. What is this power that doctors have over us? Few other people have the ability to make me so nervous. John Cusack springs to mind, but only because he smelled that good in person. And was that tall. And because the mutual friend introducing us had threatened to present me as *Liz, who really wants to sleep with you.* I challenge any woman not to be tongue-tied in a situation like that.

"Feeding her," he repeated. "What are you feeding the baby?"

"Baby food?"

He turned towards me, eyebrows raised. I froze. Wrong answer? He flipped one hand over, palm up, and gestured for me to continue.

I drew a complete blank. What did I feed her? A series of quick MTV-like cuts flashed through my mind. The baby food aisle of the supermarket. CUT TO: Rows of identical baby food jars on the shelves. CUT TO: Our kitchen counter littered with baby food jars because we haven't yet made a place in the pantry for them. CUT TO: Blurry close-up of the baby food label from this morning's breakfast.

I could almost visualize it . . . it's coming into focus . . . a label . . . with an illustration . . . a picture of . . .

"Fruits!" I shouted like the slow contestant on *Family Feud* that the contenders dragged along as a last-minute replacement for a sick cousin. "I feed her fruits!" Toning it down a little, "And vegetables. Also cereal. A little. I mean, she's been constipated so, um—"

"No meats?"

Was I supposed to be feeding her meats? I wondered. *She has no teeth. Should she be eating pork chops? Chicken wings? Flank steak? Oh my God, I can't even cook. What meat have I ever cooked? Fajitas. I can make her fajitas. Wait, here's a better idea—maybe if I wish for it very, very hard, I will turn invisible right now.*

"Pureed meat," he clarified, reading my expression too well. "Baby foods with meat. Like chicken. You can buy them at the store."

"OK, meat. I understand. And for the constipation—"

"You're not feeding her bran? You should be feeding her bran."

"Just oatmeal and rice cereal. But like I said, we stopped because—"

"Bran."

"OK, it's just that—"

"Bran."

"I know, I just—"

"Bran."

"Well, then!" I said brightly. "Meats and bran it is!"

The doctor said nothing further; he just turned and walked out of the office giving me a halfhearted little wave over his right shoulder.

"I guess that means the appointment is over, Monkey," I told Thalia.

And then she leaned forward and put my entire nose in her mouth. I'd like to think it was her way of saying, *Don't worry, Mommy. I still think you're great.* And she couldn't have picked a better time.

LIKE REINFLATING A TIRE

Jenny Lauck THREE KID CIRCUS

Late one afternoon at Dr. Hot's office, he looked at my wilting daughter and said that he thought an IV might be in order. She was unable to keep anything down. It had been three whole days.

I stood there with one hand on my four-year-old, who was attempting to make a hasty exit from the exam room, and the other on my two-year-old, who was in the leopard-print sling, arching her back and trying to eject herself headfirst onto the floor. I swallowed hard, told the good doctor that I would sit up all night trying to hydrate my daughter, and we would return in the morning for an IV if things didn't improve.

Back at home, I held my heaving daughter through the night, forcing sips of Pedialyte down her throat and making repeated trips to the sink for cool cloths and to rinse the big bowl. By dawn, I had already discussed the IV with my girl, and while she was fearful, she was limp and just wanted to feel better.

The hubs was shaking and feverish but, hey, I handle the kids no matter the weather, so I left the two other hooligans home with my sick-as-a-dog husband and drove to the pediatrician's office. Really, my husband's timing was great, because had he been healthy, he *had* to go to the office to see the bigwigs. Glass half full! After a quick check and a couple of chest X-rays, we were put in the "procedure room" for the IV.

After my daughter demonstrated that what little fight she had left she was going to focus on keeping that needle away from her arm, I helped two nurses to swaddle her in a blanket and held her on my lap while they got the IV in place. She sobbed into my chest while they worked. Mercifully, they got it on the first try and the tears subsided quickly.

After drawing some blood for tests they got the drip going and I found myself sitting in a wooden glider chair, holding my swaddled daughter for the first time since she was an infant. Her six-year-old face is full of angles, not the soft, round, puppy folds of her baby face. Her head rested on my shoulder and her feet dangled a few inches above the floor, and I marveled at the sheer size of her. I felt like I was rocking Baby Huey.

She refused to lie on the bed. She wanted to be held, and I gladly sat in the rocker, heels keeping a rhythm, while my right arm, left leg, and entire butt went numb. I rested my cheek on her hair and I swear her scalp still smells the same as it did when she was a baby. Not quite the newborn smell, but her unique smell—I would know it anywhere.

Although it was hard initially, once we settled in and the nurses and their questions went away, we just rocked. My girl dozed, then lay quietly alert in my arms, eyes searching my face or scanning the far wall. It was so similar to her infant times when she would just chill after a big nursing session that it was eerie.

The nurses kept asking if I wanted to read, if I wanted to watch TV, if I wanted to eat or drink. I just wanted to hold my girl and be quiet. The clicking and sighing of the IV was hypnotic, and I simply sat and squeezed drops of good out of the situation. I had nothing to do but snuggle my girl. I had peace and quiet. My daughter would leave there that afternoon, rested and hydrated.

For four hours we sat there. They gave her two bags of fluids. For the last twenty minutes, she chose to lie on the bed and I stood next to her, pins and needles (or as she says, scissors and paper clips) up and down my lower half. Suddenly my Baby Huey looked tiny and pathetic. The sight of my kiddo in a hospital bed made me tear up, and we were about to leave. I hope I never have to see that again.

6

The Annoying Outside World

Most people won't walk up to a woman trying on bridal gowns and tell her she shouldn't spend twenty thousand dollars on her wedding. They won't tell an executive she should really update her haircut.

Just wait until that woman gets pregnant. Even worse, wait until the baby emerges into their neighborhood. Suddenly, everyone's a child psychologist or pediatrician. Everyone who has ever babysat for more than two hours is a childcare expert. Older women only had angelic progeny, melded not by nature or nurture but by their own iron wills. Not only do these people know everything there is to know about raising children, they have been waiting their entire, complete lives for their opportunity to tell you how to raise yours.

Not only will the outside world give you unsolicited advice, it will influence your adorable, sinless child more and more as that child grows toward adulthood. There is a temptation at, oh, about four years of age, to lock the child in his or her room and swallow the key with a nice pinot noir, often after the child first pretends to shoot you dead with a banana despite the fact you never let that child watch anything but PBS.

SINCE WHEN IS CYNICAL A BAD THING?

Kelli Oliver George RANCID RAVES

I was telling my sister the other day that I was tired of screening the same old boring pregnancy questions over and over at work and other social gatherings with people that I don't know very well (note: it's different with friends and family, for whatever reason). She claimed that I was cynical. The nerve! Just think how much more interesting life would be if we could push back all the bullshit and say what we *really* wanted to say.

Question: Did I hear you are pregnant?
Answer: Yes! (*Gushing.*)
Fantasy Answer: No. Why? Do I look pregnant?

Question: How are you feeling?
Answer: Great! (*Gushing.*)
Fantasy Answer: I am quickly realizing why everyone claims the second trimester is the "best" one where you feel "great." It's easy to say that about a trimester that is bookended by two hellish trimesters. If *this* is good, gee, I can't *wait* to hit the third one.

Question: Are you excited?
Answer: Yes! (*gushing*)

Fantasy Answer: No! I wanted new living room furniture, and instead I got *this*. (*Point to mushrooming stomach.*)

Question: Is your husband excited?
Answer: Yes! (*Gushing.*)
Fantasy Answer: What husband?

Question: What are you having?
Answer: We don't know. I haven't had a sonogram yet. (*Gushing.*)
Fantasy Answer: Rosemary's baby.

Question: Do you want a boy or a girl?
Answer: I don't care as long as it is healthy. (*Honestly.*)
Fantasy Answer: I'm hoping for a kung fu–fighting hamster.

Question: Have you picked out a name yet?
Answer: No, we are going to wait and see what the kid is first. (*Resignedly.*)
Fantasy Answer: We decided to go with something nontraditional in the form of ancient Egyptian hieroglyphics—the Baby Formerly Known as It.

Question: Is your husband going to quit traveling when the baby comes?
Answer: No, he doesn't have a choice when it comes to travel, and we like to eat. (*Resignedly.*)
Fantasy Answer: Yes. We are going to live off our credit cards for awhile and see how that works. Food, schmood.

Question: You're going to stay home with the baby? Boy, aren't you lucky?

Answer: Yes. (*Humbly.*)

Fantasy Answer: Well, I guess we were lucky as we worked our asses off through college and then got good jobs for which we worked even more. I guess we were superlucky that my husband got full-ride scholarships for his degrees, because we are feverishly trying to get *my* student loans paid off before the kid comes.

Question: Are you going to get a four-door car?

Answer: No, I am going to see how it works with the two-door because it is already paid off. It may be inconvenient, but it will be worth not having a car payment. (*Logically.*)

Fantasy Answer: The kid can't ride in the trunk?

Question: Are you going to have drugs when you give birth?

Answer: YES. (*Emphatically.*)

Fantasy Answer: *Yes,* you sadist. I had drugs when my wisdom teeth were taken out, and I damn well will have drugs for *this*.

Question: Do you have a theme for the nursery?

Answer: No. (*Emphatically.*)

Fantasy Answer: We were thinking S&M.

I THINK I'M IN THE WRONG VILLAGE
Liz Gumbinner MOM-101

It's only taken few brief months of motherhood to learn that everyone knows my child better than I do, from the gaggle of bespectacled old women who suggested rather emphatically that I should move to a table farther from the front door in the coffee shop to the considerate nanny on the street who shouted, "Get a hat on that baby!" extra loud, just to make sure I didn't miss out on some rare, free advice from a paid, professional childcare expert. What a lucky first-time mom I am to reap the expertise of the entire community. Like the saleswoman who cast a narrowed eye on Thalia then remarked, "Wow, she's a skinny one. Don't you feed her?" Well my goodness, if it weren't for you reminding me, I might have gone right on not feeding her for another three weeks. And the very same day, the neighbor who said, "Four months? She's huge! What are you feeding her?" You know, the usual. Breast milk. Chicken McNuggets.

And then there is that all-seeing, all-knowing woman in my building. Of course there is. Every big building in New York has at least one of them. In this case, she's the slick, silver-tongued, aerobicized Realtor who likes to grandstand for her open house visitors in the lobby each Sunday by greeting each resident by name and throwing out some little tidbit that demonstrates just how close she is with every one of us.

"Hi, *Liz*, hi, *Nate*. Hope you had a nice trip to *California* last week. How is your darling bulldog, *Emily*? And the baby? *Talia*? How is she? Still got those *huge, brown* eyes?"

Never mind that her name isn't Talia and I've corrected the woman, politely, sixteen times.

When I was pregnant, the woman consistently assured me there was no way I was sixteen (twenty-three, thirty-seven) weeks, because I was way too small. And not in a complimentary way, either. Rather, it was in a "get a second opinion, I could be saving the life of your fetus" way. You know, because after sixteen (twenty-three, thirty-seven) weeks of counting every minute since conception, I, along with my top-rated, high-risk Manhattan obstetrician, may have made a deadly mathematical error.

Once Thalia was born, I was lucky enough to continue running into this woman so that I could further harvest her little gems of maternal wisdom. Like the importance of getting a good night's sleep when I could. Or the innovative suggestion that if Nate shared some of the night feedings, I could sleep more. One afternoon after I returned from a walk with the baby, she cornered me in the elevator and inquired whether I was still breastfeeding. Before I could answer, she stared squarely at my triple-Ds and answered her own question.

"Well, of course you are."

Well, of course I was.

"How is it going?" she asked.

"Oh, just fine, thanks. Really no problems."

"You say that now. But just know, " Here she leaned in close to me, looking from side to side as if to dramatize the major secret she was about to reveal. "Just know that men have a very hard time with breastfeeding. They're jealous of this beautiful bonding experience between you and the baby that they can never have themselves. So if you start having some problems with your husband, just know that this is what it is."

I nodded graciously, smiling with lips pressed together just a little too tightly. The elevator doors rumbled open. For once I appreciated living on a low floor.

"Oh!" she called out from the elevator as I headed down the hallway, "That's not to say you shouldn't keep breastfeeding. It's very good for your child!"

It takes a village indeed.

TODAY WAS UNENTHUSIASTIC DAD DAY IN THE PARK

Eden Marriott Kennedy FUSSY

The scene: I am pushing Jackson in the swing as Unenthusiastic Dad (who looks vaguely like Gary Sinise) places Cute Blond Son in the next swing.

Me: *(Smile at newcomers.)* Subtext of smile: "Hi! I'm willing to chat about babies."

Cute Blond Son: *(Gives me huge smile back.)* Subtext of smile: "Wow! You're a woman! My mom's a woman, too! Women are incredible!"

Me: *(Encouraged by big reaction.)* "Hey! Look at all those teeth!" Subtext of statement: Talking about a child's teeth is a way to roughly guess his or her age, leading to further conversation about babies.

Unenthusiastic Dad: *(Bends slightly to look at son's teeth, straightens up, does not reply.)* Possible subtext of silence: (a) "Yup, he's got teeth all right"; (b) "How dare you fucking *look* at my son's teeth! I am so furious at you right now that I can't speak"; or (c) "¿Qué?"

Me: *(Silent smiling, swing pushing.)* Subtext of silence: "OK, fuck you, too."

Yes, I am about to get my period, why do you ask?

MORE BELL RINGING,
LESS CRAPPY TREATMENT

Sheryl Naimark PAPER NAPKIN

Tonight I was at Applebee's having (appropriately) an Appletini. A preschool-aged girl at a table nearby blew a gasket. Rather than trying to solve the problem, the mother felt that the most important thing was for the child to *be quiet* and *shut up*, which she emphasized by slapping her. The little girl was finally appeased by being allowed to play with the mother's cigarettes and lighter. Whatever.

The hazardous-materials-as-toys motif did not bother me (OK, I'm lying), but the mistreatment did. I think every time a child gets treated like crap, something equally tremendous happens, and not in the good way. Incidents like this break my heart. When I am someplace like the grocery store and I see a child yanked on or screamed at, it makes me so sad I could sit down in the frozen-food aisle and weep.

Don't get me wrong. I have three kids and before I had three kids I taught elementary school. I know kids are often infuriating, demanding, little button-pushers. There have been many times I have said and done things that I wished I hadn't. Things I've had to apologize for later. But no matter what evil plot they mastermind and deftly execute, they are kids. Essentially, they're powerless.

That's why I think respect is such an important part of parenting. By respect I don't mean you should abdicate and let them run the joint, which is how some parenting manuals define "respect." I'm all about benevolent dictatorships. But these are *people* with wants and needs and opinions and emotions. Those are valuable attributes I want to be aware of as I interact with my children. I don't want to just shut them up because they're making a scene and I'm embarrassed.

If your ego is leading the way, you're doomed.

I don't know whether the element of respect is present between the mother and daughter I saw tonight, and I've been a parent long enough to know that it would be a huge mistake to judge a parent's style based solely on what one can observe over an Appletini. So instead, here's a toast, "To parents everywhere. May we have a little more respect and patience tomorrow than we did today."

HAVE I EVER STEERED
YOU WRONG?

Jenifer Scharpen NOT CALM (DOT COM)

My daughter Sophie went to play at a friend's house, and the mom asked beforehand if I minded if she left the girls with her babysitter while she went to pick up her older daughter. I know the mom well enough to know she wouldn't leave her children with a total knucklehead, so I said it was fine. She said that the babysitter was a he, and was I OK with that. "Absolutely," I said. "That's fine."

The babysitter turned out to be an older (maybe in his sixties) man. He saw us come in and say hello to the girls, and asked if I was Sophie's mom. I said yes.

He asked if all those kids were mine.

"Yes. They are all mine."

"Three are yours?"

"No, four," I said.

And he said, "You are rich with children! You are so blessed!"

Do you know he was the first person I can think of who has had a genuinely positive response when he found out that I have four kids? Usually I get looked down upon, asked if I know where babies come from (you think?), or get some version of the "are *all* those kids *yours*?" question.

Often people with one or two kids will say to me something like, "Wow, I struggle with my two all the time. How do you do it with four?"

And, usually, I say something like, "Well, the hardest thing is going from zero to one. I think I was just as overwhelmed with one as I am with four. Once you have a child, *all* your time and energy goes in their direction—so it really doesn't make that much of a difference if you have one or if you have ten; parenting is all-consuming no matter how many kids you have."

I've come to realize lately that I am totally full of shit.

Was I saying that to convince myself? Who knows? What I do know is that some weekday mornings all four kids have to get out the door by eight, and other mornings it's just the boys. The days when just the boys have to go are pretty peaceful: the getting dressed, eating, lunch packing, brushing, and flossing happen pretty seamlessly, as a rule. Of course they gripe and moan and forget their lunches and homework and such, but compared to the days when everyone must be woken up, dressed, fed, brushed, shod, and jacketed, while finding their sharing/library books/backpack/permission slips, the days with two are markedly easier than the days with four.

Now, it may be that I'd never have noticed that it was easy with two if I didn't have four to hold up as a glaring comparison. After all, when Lex was a baby, I looked at people with two or three kids and freaked out a little at the very idea of having more than one child. I so clearly remember being pregnant with Nathan and talking to a mom at the park who'd just had her third child. I was pumping her for information because I couldn't believe that I was going to be able to handle two kids. Several years later, she was marveling at me, saying how she was coping with her three but couldn't imagine having four.

My older three kids do spend every other weekend with their dad and stepmom, so I get breaks that most mothers of four do not.

Every time they go, I resolve to clean the house and get little projects that I've been putting off forever taken care of, but usually I shift into low gear. I putter (what a luxury—I wish I'd appreciated the fine art of puttering more when I had free access to it), I read, I cook, and we take Willow out to places that are sort of a pain with all the kids.

I don't know if I'll cry in my beer the next time someone asks me if it's really tough having four kids, but I think I'll stop sugarcoating it.

A DEAD LANGUAGE MAY
JUST KILL ME

Lisa Stone SURFETTE

Now that my son is nine, I've been stunned by a new behavior when he and his posse are together. Suddenly, Pokemon cards and Legos are on the outs. The boys sit around and *talk*. Sometimes, they even whisper.

Uh-oh. Now I'm waiting for the smack upside the head that my son is a genuine tween, preparing to disappear off the cliff of adolescence. There are signs. He's already asked when he can get a mohawk, what I would think if he tattooed his face, and what a condom is. But I can tell he's just testing me. He doesn't really want them. Yet.

I know what I'm looking for—a very precise harbinger of hormones from my own past: Latin. Anatomically correct Latin, that is. I know he's going to use it. What worries me is how.

My son has some experience in this field. At age almost-three, when he was trying to figure out why his little friend Sarah was a girl and he was a boy, he got his first lesson in underpants Latin. I sat him right down with a cartoon book for little ones and executed what I assured myself was a matter-of-fact anatomy lesson. "Well, that's that!" I congratulated myself. "The Talk will be no problem for *moi!*"

There's nothing like Mother Nature to bring a girl down a peg. A few days later, the flaws in my teaching moment were revealed, as so many things are, in the frozen-food section of the local grocery. As I rounded the corner of one aisle, my son looked up at me from the front seat of the grocery cart, where he had been playing with his seatbelt. "Mommy?" he inquired, in that loud, piercing outside voice he favored those days. I 'scuse-me'd past the cart of an older man who was waist-deep into the ice cream, his back to us. I was headed for the pie. ""Uh-huh, baby?" I said as I opened the freezer to check out the goods.

"So you're saying that men have a penis, and women have a buh-gina?" his little voice reached a fabulous high note on each anatomically correct term.

The oh-so-close haunches of the guy with his head in the freezer froze. *Don't laugh, don't laugh, don't you dare laugh, you stupid smug idiot*, I told myself, *or he'll be saying penis and vagina at every family gathering for the next ten years, and everyone will know who's fault that is, won't they?*

The man was still in the freezer. He looked like he would stay there forever rather than turn around so that his penis faced my buh-gina.

"Yes!" I shouted, throwing pies back into the freezer. "Where is that cookie aisle?"

We escaped without forcing the poor guy to make eye contact and the issue died. Until three years later, when my son's stepmother was expecting another baby.

"Mom, I just don't get where babies come from," he told me one day when I picked him up from first grade. "And don't tell me about the sperm and the egg again, because I've heard it all before. I just don't get how the sperm and the egg *get* in the same place." However, he assured me, he knew all about how babies were born.

"How, son?"

"They come out where the mom poops," he reported. "Everyone knows that, Mom."

Out came a different book, a 1973 illustrated version of *Where Do Babies Come From?* that my clairvoyant mother had mailed to me that very month. I swore my son to a blood pact: what I was about to show him was never, ever to be discussed in the frozen-food aisle.

He was shocked, to say the least. "Daddy did that?" he asked. I was a little shell-shocked myself. I couldn't believe I was discussing sex at all. As a single mom, I was apparently permanently dateless and never going to get a chance to indulge in the act of sex again, much less have a baby.

We talked a lot of Latin that afternoon. I should have known that would come back to haunt me. Because that's the thing about my son: he likes to talk, just like his mother. And he likes to try out his new words. As he did the very next day, as soon as he got into the car.

"Oh, Mom! You packed me too much lunch today!" he said.

"I did?" I said. "You actually ate it, for once?"

"Yeah!" said my son. "I ate it all! And later my intesticles were killing me!"

Have you ever seen a station wagon with coffee spewed inside the windshield? If I ever have an aneurysm, I will credit the effort it took not to bray with laughter that day.

"Ummm, honey, there are two words that sound a lot alike but they actually do very different things, " I began.

Flash forward to today and my fears. These innocent questions are not the anatomically correct Latin that worries me. I'm on guard against a misappropriation of the terms, and the private parts to which they refer. Because at tweendom, I think, boys begin the lifelong process of deciding how to treat girls. As other humans, or as less-than-equals. Or, worse yet, as objects or even things. And I worry about this.

I was nine the first time I heard Latin thus abused and knew it for what it was. I was sitting in Mrs. Lizotte's fifth-grade class in Missoula, Montana, hating every hair of her beehive. Happily, to my right sat serious entertainment. Lauren, the smartest boy in the class, spent his days turning around to hatch trouble with his buddy, David, the toughest boy in the class.

David could do crazy playground tricks like turn his eyelids inside out. Earlier that year, they'd thrilled us all by loosening the bolts on Lizotte's ancient wooden office chair, damn near maiming her.

I snuck a peek at David. He grinned at me, the blood-red undersides of his eyelids popping.

"Ew!" I was delighted.

Lauren turned around, his math long done, and let us have it.

"David, you clitoris," Lauren hissed.

I gasped. I rubbernecked at David—could he possibly know what that meant? Oh yeah, he did. And from the smirk on his face, I could tell it wasn't the first time he'd heard it. David laughed. Lauren laughed.

Then they looked at my burning face, my mouth hanging open in shock. And howled.

There it was—my first experience hearing males use female anatomy to insult each other. Pow. I cannot count the number of times I heard that word on the playground that year, or how many kids clearly knew what it meant. Lauren went on to call all of us "scrotum" at one point or another too, but it never had the same effect.

I had an immediate change of heart about old Lizotte, who clamped down on them, ended the discussion, and made it possible for me to start breathing again. Little did she or I realize, it was a girl-bonding moment.

It took a decade for me to figure out why I was so horrified and humiliated by the particular use of that term as an insult. Of course, I didn't understand then like I do now the role that the clitoris plays for women worldwide, both in pleasure and in pain (female circumcision anyone? Yes, I will judge that cultural value).

Now let's be clear—I don't think my fifth-grade classmates understood the deeper implications of what they were doing. Hell, they insulted each other all day long. But it was the way they used their shocking new word that rattled me. A lot went unnoticed then for which my son knows I'd cheerfully roast him alive today.

But I learned something. Sit down with any sitcom or movie or computer game today, and I'll bet good money that we can identify a number of moments where the ultimate insult delivered to men is that they are female in some way. And the worst insult is still for one male to call another a buh-gina.

So I'm on the lookout for telltale signs that my sweet, caring son, who has always had female friends and, Lord knows, a strong maternal figure in his life, is heading to the dark side.

As I said, I know he's going to use these terms. What worries me is how. Because that's when the dead language, Latin, may just kill me.

7

Kids Can Be Difficult

One of the chief reasons I was drawn to the blogosphere (and these writers in particular) is honesty. I read all the parenting authors. There were a few (Vicki Iovine comes to mind) who admitted to hating a nursing bra or the extra flap of skin above the belly button that never, ever goes away. But immediately after admitting something to this effect, the author would immediately gush how it was all worth it, how every inconvenience and physical pain was worth this beautiful, precious child.

Well, of course it was worth it! But that doesn't mean that children don't sometimes really suck.

I ATE PILLS

Kristen Chase MOTHERHOOD UNCENSORED

I admit to having a few anxiety issues, but I managed to laugh, cry, giggle, and obsess my way through most of life without any major breakdowns. However, the combination of raging hormones, having a kid, and having free, unlimited access to Google has driven me near the brink of insanity. You know what I mean. Your kid coughs and rubs her eyeballs about three times in a row, and you're rushing to Google to find out what the hell is wrong with her—only to learn that it could be anything from late-stage AIDS to chronic asthma. Or just allergies. Or maybe nothing at all.

And so, my anxiety levels are piqued. I'm a pinging ball of frazzle, just waiting to explode.

A few days ago, my two-year-old daughter had moved from "my zone" to the "huz's zone" (it's similar to zone defense, except we get paid way less and don't get any cheerleaders). However, he seems to forget her penchant for getting into things and, lo and behold, when I found her, she had opened up my large makeup case. And next to her was a bag of multivitamins.

I made no effort not to freak out. Sure, the bag was sealed tightly, but still. She could have opened it, swallowed five large, disgusting, pink pills, and then zipped it back up with her perfect two-year-old finger dexterity.

I lost it.

"Did you see her with these pills?" I screamed. "Did she eat the pills?"

"Um. No, honey. I don't think she did," my husband replied, not even looking up from the television.

"Hello. She could die *right now!*" I screamed, frantically trying to find the number for Poison Control.

So I asked her. "Quinlan, did you eat these pills?"

"Uh-huh," she replied, applying a thick layer of red lipstick to her forehead.

"*What*? How many did you eat?"

She pointed to her mouth. "One, two, three, four, five ..." She continued to about fifteen, her maxed-out counting number of late.

"Are you sure you ate them, honey?"

"Uh-huh."

I continued to whip around the house in a flurry, now trying to stop my husband from leaving for work with one hand while calling information and then Poison Control with my other. My phone was still wet from its juice dive the day before, and it kept cutting out. *She's dying right now*, I thought, *and I can't get my free piece-of-shit phone to work. I'm going to hell.*

While my husband drove to work and called Poison Control, I ran to my daughter. Before I could ask her anything, she came to me with her face painted red and a sweet cheery voice, saying, "I ate pills, Mama. I ate pills!"

"What? No, no, no, no."

That was all I needed to begin what could only have been cut straight out of *Law & Order: Mothers in Need of Xanax.*

"Did you eat Daddy's mouthwash?" I asked, holding the bottle up for her to see.

"Uh-huh," she replied, matter of factly.

"OK. How about Mommy's foot scrubber? Did you eat that too?"

"Uh-huh," she nodded, like she knew what a foot scrubber was and had used it several times before.

"OK. Now open this bag. Now. Open it!" I screamed, shaking it rapidly in front of her face.

She couldn't do it. So I did it and offered her the pills.

"Eat this! Mommy wants you to eat one now." I forced a pill into her mouth only to have her spit it out, barely able to place it on her tongue.

"Now close the bag. *Close it!*"

She tried valiantly, obviously trying to please her distraught mother, but she couldn't get any type of seal—probably because she's two and can't seal a sandwich bag.

But even after all that, plus the reassuring call from my husband saying that she would be fine unless she ate more than ten, you would think I'd have full confidence that she did not eat the pills. But, thanks to being juiced up on mommy hormones, I didn't.

All day long, thanks to what could only be described as extremely bad karma, my daughter would not stop chanting "I ate pills right der," while pointing into her open mouth. And in my head, all I could hear was "I need pills. I need pills right der," pointing to my own open mouth.

I certainly learned my lesson. Now I keep the Poison Control phone number handy—written in huge black numbers on the big bottle of "Mommy pills."

PITY THE PARENTS
Tracey Gaughran-Perez SWEETNEY

On Saturday, Jamie, Mina, and I decided to brave the oppressive, stifling heat and motor down to our neighborhood cafe and bookstore for a light supper. And let me begin my tale by saying to every childless person who reads this: pity the parents you see out with a toddler, baby, or preschooler who chooses to *lose their freakin' shit* at a restaurant. No, those parents did not know that this was going to happen, and no, they aren't purposefully trying to spoil your relaxing and drama-free dining experience. They are *mortified*, and just as annoyed as you are (if not more so), so rather than shoot fiery deathrays from your eyes at them as they attempt to restrain their whining, screeching, flailing child, why not employ some simple human empathy and kindly avert your gaze from the horrifying spectacle unfolding before you? Is that really so much to ask? Huh?

So you see where this is going.

Within moments of arriving at the cafe, Mina spilled three-quarters of a full eight-ounce glass of apple juice on her shoes. That, my friends, was a *warning shot*. But, feeling lucky or stupidly optimistic, we decided to clean her up and move on to the fresh hell of Round Two: Solid Foods. Presented with her meal, Mina did everything but actually consume any of it. She waved her peanut butter and jelly sandwich around her head threateningly, like a cocked pistol. She smeared wads of peanut butter and gobs of jelly onto the table. She gyrated in her chair as though in full seizure, refusing to be still for even the most fleeting of moments. And *the whining,* OH THE WHINING. Jamie and I took turns shoveling food in our mouths while one of us manned the Tilt-A-Whirl molded into the shape of our daughter, alternately growling behavioral corrections and pleading with her to *please stop the insanity.* After about ten minutes of this, Jamie lifted Mina out of her chair, looked me in the eye, and said in his best *I'm calm, dammit!* voice, "We're leaving. I'll meet you out front."

Good times.

So I gathered our things, muttered some vague apologies to the cafe owner, and scurried out the front door, to-go cup of iced coffee in hand.

Sometimes, when bad things happen, it seems that space-time perceptibly alters: the environment becomes visibly heightened and ultravivid, with each moment excruciatingly prolonged, each movement in slow motion. And then there are times when badness descends like an anvil: so swiftly that it is experienced only as a shapeless blur of an instant, as when you gracelessly tumble down a full flight of concrete stairs outside your neighborhood cafe, landing with a tremendous *smack* on top of the splattered remains of your to-go cup of iced coffee.

Ow. Ow. Ow.

Every appendage was scratched, cut, and bleeding in some form or fashion. I felt like a piñata that had just gone through the merciless ringer of a preschooler's birthday party.

Managing, with some difficulty, to stand up, I hobbled to the car, crying and moaning "Ow! Ow! Ow!" with rhythmic repetition. Once inside our car, Mina—having apparently regained her senses—

gently put one tiny hand on my shoulder from the back seat in an attempt to console me. "It's OK, Mommy. It was an accident." *Pat pat pat.*

Accident? What is she talking about? *Those stairs were trying to kill me.*

I JUST HAVE TO FIGURE OUT HOW HE PRINTED THIS

Alice Bradley FINSLIPPY

I found the following tucked away in a corner of Henry's crib. I am so onto him.

Date: April 1, 2005
To: Child 4A0765B-1007@children.com, toddler_unit@children.com
From: Kevin, VP, Toddler Division
Subject: Quarterly Objectives

Happy new year, company members! As you know, our first quarter was a fruitful and productive one. By working together to delay our bedtimes, we acquired over 53,000 extra hours of valuable awake time. That's 53,000 more hours of running in circles; 53,000 more hours of shaking our heads wildly and arching our backs; 53,000 more hours of the parents straining to communicate that toothbrushes do not go in the diaper. We have seen the parents falter and ultimately give way under our consistent efforts, and we are proud.

It should be mentioned that some of our members have made great strides in drastically limiting the variety of foodstuffs they allow to enter their face-holes. We are thinking especially of Child 3A0762C-0908, who now ingests only raisins and lukewarm water sipped from a plastic spork; Child 5B0755F-0528, ketchup on crackers and the occasional mashed grape; and, most breathtakingly,

Child 8A0576L-0108, plain dried breadcrumbs licked off a moistened index finger.

For the second quarter, we've strengthened our resolve and shown what a little determination and a lot of screeching can accomplish. And we are ready for the next phase: Operation No Pants.

Every morning without failing, the caregivers initiate a dressing procedure that is tiresome at best and scratchy at worst. It distracts us from our viewing of Elmo and limits our access to our smooth, smooth skin. Their motives are puzzling: either they are jealous of our smooth, smooth skin or else are attempting to break our wills by imposing nonsensical rules and demanding that we comply. But they will not succeed, friends. Because we will resist.

No matter how sopping wet or poop crammed your diaper is, refuse to allow your caregiver to remove it. Declare that diaper to be your *favorite* diaper. Do not allow any larger beings to lay a finger on it. For motivation, imagine that said diaper is part of your body, like a real tushie over your tushie. If any attempt is made to remove it, you will scream. Remember: the scream is your friend. Caregivers live in fear of the scream.

If you add to the scream "No hit! No hit!", they're sure to back away for fear of the authorities coming after them.

Declare your opinions at each and every turn, and make sure that they are as vague and baffling as your pronunciation. If your caregiver explains that dressing is a vital step in a traveling-to-playground initiative, screech, "Murfy! *Too murfy!*" Do not explain. Never explain.

But why do we resist, you ask? Why not get dressed and enter the playground, where fun could possibly be had? Because, that's why. Because, because, because. Because we must take every stand we are able to take. Also! Because your caregiver is deceiving you. There is another, better playground, a naked playground, with balloons and ice cream and cake. The soiled diaper will lead the way. This is true, we think.

Onward!

Kevin

ARE YOU THERE, GOD? IT'S ME, RISA

Risa Green MOMMY TRACK'D

I know, I know, it's been a while. Anyway, in case you don't remember me, I'm the one who doesn't really like people all that much. I mean, not all people, of course, I like my friends, and some of my family, I just don't like the really annoying people with whom You seemed to populate most of the world (and dude, what is up with that?). I think You know who I'm talking about. That one supermarket checker who always tries to chat me up about my cheese selection. Strangers in elevators who feel compelled to talk during a thirty-second ride. People in restaurants who sit next to me and eavesdrop, and then try to join in on my conversation. I mean, I'm just not interested, you know?

But about that, I do want to say thank you for a few things. 1) Thanks for making my husband. There are very few people I could live with, let alone live with every single day for the rest of my life, and so it was cool of You to make someone who is almost as misanthropic as I am. Do you know what he said the other day? I was feeling kind of loner-like, even for me, and so I suggested that we should maybe make plans with this couple who we kind of know but haven't ever really gone out with. Totally out of character, I know. But he said, "Honey, I already have enough friends. I don't need any more. And do you really feel like having another person whom you'll have to talk to on the phone?"

And I was like, "You are so right. I don't know what I was thinking."

And so anyway, thanks for that. 2) Thanks for the whole writer gig. I mean, no annoying coworkers, no office politics, no sucking up to a boss. I just get to sit in a room, by myself, for six hours a day, and get paid for it. How great is that? A brilliant move. I really, really, appreciate it.

So do you remember me now? You do? OK, so then what is up with giving me the friendliest freakin' kid ever? Huh? What is that about? I mean, You made me the way that I am, right? And You made my husband the way that he is. And presumably, You thought we were a pretty good match. So then what makes You think that we would know what to do with a kid who talks to every single person in the universe? Every single one, God. Every. Single. One. Now, OK, yes, sometimes, it's cute. Like the other day, when she told some random lady at the dry cleaners that she just bought two new ballet dresses and that she's going to wear the pink one this week and the white one next week, and then she'll wear the pink one again, so it'll be like a pattern: pink, white, pink, white, pink, white. I'll admit, it made me smile. But most of the time it just totally freaks me out. I mean, it is against my nature, You know?

Like that time when she was three, and we were outside on the balcony, having a tea party. She heard our neighbor across the street come home, and my instinct was to duck down and hide, which was exactly what I did. But then Little Miss Social Butterfly stands up and starts yelling at the top of her lungs. "Hi, neighbor! I'm having a tea party with my mommy. She's right here, but you can't see her because she's hiding. But it's not really tea, it's just water, but we're pretending it's tea, even though I don't really like tea, I like lemonade better. Mommy, can it be a lemonade party instead of a tea party?"

I was so busted, and I had to stand up and pretend that I wasn't hiding, ha, ha, ha, and then I had to make small talk for ten minutes with my neighbor, who's nice and everything, but I think we've already established how I feel about small talk.

And what about that time last week, when we were going for a walk in the neighborhood, and we saw some friends of hers from school and their nannies. They were totally on the other side of the street, at least fifty feet ahead, and in a million years they would never have known that we were behind them, which was just fine with me. But there goes my kid, chasing after them, waving, and somehow I end up with all of them in my house: me, three kids, and two nannies who don't speak a lick of English. And now I'm forced not only to make small talk, but to make small talk in a foreign language. I mean, come on, God. Is Depeche Mode right about you? Do you really have a sick sense of humor?

When people ask us who she takes after, we have no idea what to say. The only thing we've been able to come up with is that maybe it's like math, when two negatives make a positive. Now, I don't know if You're punishing me for something, or if this is Your way of telling me that I should maybe be a little nicer to people, or maybe a little less intolerant of total morons, like that old lady yesterday who I screamed at for not staying in her lane, but I'm here to tell You that I've gotten the message, *loud and clear*. OK? And look, what's done is done. She is who she is, You can't change her now, blah, blah, blah. I get it. And so all I'm asking for is this: when she's old enough, can you at least just try to make sure that she has a well-developed sense of sarcasm? Because I don't really think that I could deal with a literal-minded kid.

Are we cool? Great.

Thanks a lot, God.

Risa

IF RICHARD III HAD A FOUR-YEAR-OLD

Doug LAID-OFF DAD

Every once in a while Robert launches in with a grandiose proclamation, but he's struck with such aphasia that he can't finish his sentence. He's worked so hard to land our attention that he's genuinely taken aback when he finally succeeds.

Now, I'm not one to lay blame on somebody who can't finish a sentence. I do it all the time. But I'm forty-one going on ninety, and in my day I was something of a weed enthusiast. What's his excuse?

It's also important to note that conversations like the one below usually occur when I'm late for something, or I really have to take a leak, or in some other situation when it's really not in my best interest to hang around and wait for the last, ornery syllable to fall.

Robert: "I want to go to . . . uh . . ."

Me: "Where?"

Robert: "Um . . . I want to go to . . . uh . . ."

Me: "Where would you like to go?"

Robert: "I want . . . uh . . . to go . . . uh . . . tooooooo . . ."

At this point, I want very damn desperately to help him fill in his blanks. But I know I'll come off like I'm hectoring him, which can't be a good thing. So to help me bite my tongue, I wander off into my own Mental MadLibs.

Robert: "I want to go . . . tooooo . . . "

Me: *The coffee shop? The hardware store? Tony n' Tina's Wedding?*

Robert: "I want to . . . go . . . to . . . "

Me: *Extremes? Great lengths? The dogs? The video tape? The bathroom?*

Robert: "I want . . . to . . . uh . . . "

Me: *Go . . . to . . .*

Robert: "Go . . . to . . . "

Me: *Uh . . .*

Robert: "Uh . . . "

Me: *Lake Michigan? Suriname? The United Arab Emirates? What, child? WHAT?*

Robert: "I forget."

My kingdom for a direct object.

ABOUT THOSE PUPPIES

Eden Marriott Kennedy FUSSY

Thursday night, when it was time to read books with Jackson before bed, I picked out a small pile of stories I thought might interest him: *One Fish, Two Fish, Red Fish, Blue Fish*, a couple of old Golden Books, a Shrek comic based on the movie but about ten times more surreal, and *Curious George and the Puppies*, which is a post–H. A. and Margret Rey Curious George book put out by a faceless committee that appears to enjoy portraying George as some sort of branding solution with aggregated cross-platform framework angles (i.e., let's get his face on as many lunchboxes as possible and screw the story line).

We'd just seen the Curious George movie, so Jackson wanted me to read the Curious George first. Then, as he gets all snuggled into his pillows, he says, real chatty-like, "Sometimes I like to hurt dogs."

Sometimes I like to shove lit firecrackers up cats' asses, Mom. Would you hand me the remote, please? Seriously. And I'm all, this is the first sign that he's going to turn into a serial killer. Likes to torture animals. I'm raising the Iceman.

But I keep it cool. Because if you freak out about the freakiness the kid will begin to hide and thus intensify the freakiness, and we don't want a pet torturer on our hands. So I just calmly asked, "Why?"

And he says, "I don't know. I just can't help it. There's something inside that makes me do it. I can't stop."

Here's where my left arm goes numb and I need a warm blanket and a defibrillator.

"Are you angry at dogs?" I ask. I don't even know where I'm going with this. I just want him to keep talking so I can look at this from all angles, possibly under the guidance of a professional.

"Just read the story, Mom."

So I read a few pages of Curious George and the Puppies, but I'm so distracted I'm not even listening to myself. I'm one-quarter panicked, one-quarter wondering where the hell he heard the phrase there's something inside that makes me do it, and fully one-half disgusted at the fact that this pleasant little rip-off of a book has no sense of the anarchic narrative magic that the original stories had. I wonder if Jackson's a little bored, too, because he interrupts me to tell me again that he agrees with Roger Ebert, although personally I think the movie would have had wider appeal if it was live action and Will Ferrell actually flew over a lion's den clutching two dozen giant balloons with a chimp clinging to his face.

And then I have to admit, when I have thoughts about how entertaining it would be to see Will Ferrell eaten by wild animals? I can sort of see where Jackson gets it from.

Anyway, we're getting toward the end of the book now, and I think it's clear by now that underneath my stoic exterior I am COMPLETELY DISTURBED by what my four-year-old son has revealed to me. But I can't help it, I need to hear more.

"So, how do you like to hurt dogs?"

"Oh, I just jump on them, or pat them real hard on the head, or squeeze their ears."

"Like when you squeezed Katie's ears that one time and she yelped?"

"Not that much, just a little bit, like this." He demonstrates with a slight pinch on my arm. I know he's not giving me the full-strength pinch. He knows I'm starting to freak out; neither of us is telling the other one the truth. So I just barrel forward and tell him that if I ever see him hurting a dog, I will stop him until he learns to stop himself. I'm quoting almost verbatim from *Touchpoints*, and I don't even care. He shrugs.

I grudgingly read the last two pages of *Curious George and the Puppies*, where the director of the animal shelter asks George if he'd like to take a puppy home, and George sure would!

And Jackson says, "I hope he hurts it."

By this point I'm really, *WTF, little man*! I was frankly pissed off, and I refused to read him any more stories. I just sat there in his bed with him, brooding, until he fell asleep on my faithless arm.

I told Jack about it the next day and he said, "He's yanking your chain."

I'm all, "You think so?" And Jack just nodded and looked at me sadly, a look that said my life is going to be sheer hell when this boy becomes a teenager.

The next day I asked Jackson if he still thought about hurting dogs, and he said, "No?" with that little up-talk swing, like, *What the hell are you talking about, Mom?* And then he skipped to the playground with his Spider-Man blanket to help make a tent with three neighborhood girls.

My God. Jackson is in preschool. He knows all the state capitals of the original thirteen colonies, and he will bluff me until I'm on the verge of brief reactive psychosis. And then he fell asleep hugging my arm.

So either I'm raising a little Ted Bundy, or I'm raising a normal little boy who is totally honest with me about the vagaries of his growing heart and mind.

Or he's just fucking with me.

But I've still got my eye on you, buddy.

Monday Morning Update

I asked him again this morning if he still thought about hurting dogs, and he laughed and said, "Yes! I still like to hurt dogs!"

So I was all, "You know that's not right, right?" And then I thought of something. "Are you scared of dogs?" I asked.

And he says, "Yes!"

"Is that why you think about hurting them?"

"Yes!"

So we went through a list of every dog I could think of to find out which ones he was scared of.

"Are you scared of Katie?"

"No."

"Oreo?"

"No."

"Are you scared of Jasmine?"

"No."

"Daisy? José? Tyson? Angel? Rocky?"

"No, no, no."

"So who *are* you scared of?" I asked.

He said, and I quote, "Big dogs with fangs coming down."

"Like you see on TV?"

"Yes. Or in your imagination."

My son wants to hurt imaginary dogs. Today. That's the story today. We may find out more tomorrow; I can't decide whether to pick this scab until it bleeds or let it fall off by itself.

MAMA, WHO INVENTED THE SPECULUM?

Miriam Kamin WOULDA COULDA SHOULDA

It was an unfortunate intersection of events. 1) My gynecologist's office decided that I am not allowed to get a new prescription for my beloved hormone patches via phone call; a check-up would be required, and 2) My sitter had to cancel.

C'mon, kids! We're going to the gyno! Everybody pick a toy and a blindfold!

When I was called back, we three trooped through the door, two of us discussing the relative merits of being able to touch one's tongue to the tip of one's nose. I'll just be mysterious about who didn't partake in that important debate.

In the exam room, the nurse offered to fetch a second chair, and I thanked her. I arranged Chickadee in the existing chair and told Monkey the next chair would be for him. The nurse returned, and I took the offered chair and faced it toward the wall, back to the exam table.

"Hey! All I can see is the wall!" complained Monkey.

"Right. That's all you need to see. Remember? I told you I'm going to have to undress, and you don't need to watch." He threw himself into the chair with a noisy sigh, and commenced tossing his stuffed puppy against the wall over and over.

"Puppy says the wall is hard!" he declared. "'Ouch!' says Puppy!"

"I get to watch," Chickadee offered to her little brother, disappointed to see him recovering so quickly. "Because Mama and I are *both* girls. You're a boy, so you don't get to. I get to see Mama's boobs."

The nurse tried to stifle a giggle (she was, by this time, taking my blood pressure). I wondered what would be the politically correct thing to say at this time. Instead, the first thing that popped into my head fell out of my mouth. "Yep, you get to see my boobs. *Wow!* You are so *lucky!*" Chickadee rolled her eyes at me. She is far too cool for my boobs, of course.

The nurse finished up and directed me to undress, don the attractive paper shirt, and cover my lower half with the paper sheet. She pulled the curtain and left the room. I told Monkey to keep his eyes on that wall while I disrobed, and he immediately squinched up his entire face and started shouting, "Are you *there*? I can't *see* anything! Where did you all *go*?" (I've gotta say, that's the first time shedding my clothes has evoked that reaction from a guy.)

I stripped down and folded up my clothes as hastily as I could, pulling on the paper shirt. "Mama," said Chickadee with a raised eyebrow, "There is no *way* that's going to cover you all up!" Seriously, she had a point. How much more would it cost them to use gowns instead of shirts? I plunked my butt down on the edge of the table. I told Monkey he could open his eyes or turn around now, but he continued weaving his torso from side to side like a tiny, inebriated Stevie Wonder, calling out, "Where are you?"

"We left!" Chickadee answered, just before slingshotting him with a ponytail holder she'd removed from her doll's hair.

The doctor arrived, fussed over the kids, looked over my chart and asked me when my last Pap smear was. "Ummm, I don't know. Isn't that my file?" That may have been the wrong answer. But she looked in the folder some more and decided it had been a while.

(Side note: I'd always thought that after a complete hysterectomy, you got the Get Out of Pap Smears Free card. I was wrong! Did you know you can actually get cancer of the vaginal wall? Yes! You can! So Pap smears are a good idea even for the cervixless. Though it still *totally* creeps me out for my doctor to cheerfully bring up my vaginal walls as if we're talking about home remodeling and not, you know, my crotch.)

This was when the doctor grew shifty eyed. She looked back and forth between the two kids (who were now discussing how Chickadee's dolly had broken her leg) and me and finally mouthed, "Are you dating?"

I found this bizarre. I mean, I wasn't thinking. I nodded, thinking that she was just extremely sensitive to the adjustment of post-divorce kids. Which would be impressive, really. But her eye darting continued and I realized *why* she was asking at about the same time that she mouthed, "And are you . . ." and here she simply stopped and made the "and so on" gesture with her hands.

I burst out laughing so hard that I nearly fell off the table.

This, of course, distracted the children from their game, and they wanted to know what was so funny, and I had to start saying things like, "Oh, look! A blood pressure cuff!" or "Wow, what a pretty mobile there is in here! It had stars, and moons, and, um, things!" And of course all of this was done while trying to stifle my laughter and my overwhelming sense of high school déjà vu.

The kids settled back into whatever they were doing, but the doctor's eyes were still darting around. "I just don't know, with them here, if we can—" she stopped. "I mean, we need to—" again, she trailed off. She tried another tactic. "HPV is a very serious—"

"Right. Well, I've never tested positive."

"But it can lay dormant for *years*," she said, in a tone of voice that indicated that I was probably dying of cervical cancer *right now* even though I no longer actually have a cervix. "You should really be tested."

"Um, OK, that's fine. Whatever."

"I have to go to the bathroom!" announced Monkey. Perfect. There was a bathroom attached to the exam room. He headed off to the bathroom while the doctor asked me to lie back and let her do a breast exam.

I did the standard hokeypokey moves for her (arm up! arm down! other arm up! now down! shake it all about, or something!) while she felt around and admired my lumpectomy scar. I pointed out that actually, I have a mammogram in a couple of weeks, so did we really need to do this? Apparently we still did, yes.

She finished up with that, and Monkey was still in the bathroom, so she had me put my feet in the stirrups and slide down while I said a small prayer that Monkey was taking his time.

At this point, the doctor snapped on her gajillion-watt lamp, trained right on my crotch, and Chickadee suddenly decided that this was plenty more interesting than her doll. She leaned forward in her chair and craned her neck to have a look between my legs.

"What's *that*?" she said with a mixture of horror and fascination when the doc whipped out the speculum. The doctor obligingly explained that it would hold the area open while she checked to make sure that I was "all healthy in there." Chickadee was transfixed as the doctor did the Pap smear.

"Is she?" asked Chickadee.

"Is she what, honey?" asked the doctor.

"All healthy in there!" she demanded. Stupid doctor.

"Oh!" She chuckled. "Well, we send this to the lab to be looked at under a microscope, but it looks good!" Chickadee nodded, satisfied that the answer was acceptable.

And then we heard a small sob from the bathroom.

"Monkey?" I was still in the stirrups, still being palpated for, well, who knows what, really. I tend not to ask many questions while someone with latex gloves is sticking their hands in me. "What's the matter, sweetie?"

Monkey responded with an agonized stream of words that sounded like, "I tried to blahblahblah and then the blahblahblah and also my poop is stuck!"

I was unclear on several parts, but decided I could address the end and fake the rest. "I'm almost done in here, sweetie. Just sit there for a minute and relax, maybe you'll get unstuck."

"OK." He sounded small and pitiful, and I mentally willed the doctor to *hurry up*, already. But now she was reading what I'd told the nurse about how I'm having heat intolerance issues and wanted to discuss changing my hormones and having my thyroid checked and, lady, I do not need to be having this discussion while I'm half-naked with my feet in stirrups and my son is sniffling in the bathroom.

Finally she wandered off to find me some samples of estrogen gel (I'm thinking of using it in my hair for better curl definition and bone density!) and told me I could get dressed. I got my clothes on as quickly as I could and went into the bathroom.

Monkey sat on the toilet kicking his legs, as if he was waiting for a bus rather than hanging out on the can in a gynecologist's office. As soon as I walked in, he pointed at the clothing bunched around his ankles. "My stupid underwear is wet."

"Don't say stupid," I replied, automatically. "Why are your undies wet?"

"I didn't point down enough. And now my undies are weeeeeet." He was sniffling again, because, you know, six-and-a-half is *big* and any time he feels less than big, it's very hard for him to take. I knew instantly what had happened, because I've seen him do it before. He sat down on the toilet and saw something shiny and just completely neglected to aim for that first second. No biggie.

"Don't cry, honey. Look, your shorts are still dry. Let's just take your undies off. No big deal." This was a thrilling solution. He gave me his underpants, and I left the bathroom in time to receive a plain brown paper bag full of samples. I tucked the paper-towel-wrapped underwear into the bag. I could hear Monkey washing his hands, and finally he emerged.

As we were buckling ourselves into the car, Chickadee asked, "So how come they have to look in there, really?" I toyed with possible answers.

"Oh, you know, it's just to make sure everything's healthy, like the doctor said." I glanced at her in the rearview mirror to see if I was going to be required to say more. She appeared to be thinking about this.

"In *where*?" asked Monkey. I sighed.

"In Mama's *vagina*!" crowed Chickadee. "They doctor *looks* in there and then uses a giant *Q-tip* to check it all out! It was *so gross*!"

Monkey considered this. I was about to begin damage control when the situation self-rectified.

"Hey, Mama?" said Monkey. "Does Chickadee know I'm not wearing any underwear?"

"Well I do *now*. Goober." The giggling commenced, and the rest of the conversation as we rode home was blessedly vagina free.

8

Memorize These Moments

So despite the physical and emotional duress, the total and complete humiliation, and the loss of some of our friends, our free time, and our discretionary income, the human race continues to exist. We keep having babies. Lots of them. Over and over. Why?

Read on.

HERE, I WROTE DOWN SOME LONG-WINDED PONTIFICATIONS ON MOMMYHOOD FOR YOU

Amy Corbett Storch AMALAH

(And while I do need to fact-check this, I'm writing from the assumption that no one in the history of the universe has ever had a baby except for me.)

Jason and I were having a discussion (over dinner) (in a restaurant) (eating food that we could cook at home, but why, when paying for it is so much fun?) (and also when it inspires the wrath of the U WENT BACK 2 WORK BECAUSE U R A SELFISH WHORE people) (and let's not forget the wine, the delicious, delicious wine) about whether or not we feel "different" since Noah was born four months ago.

I immediately chimed in with a *Raising-Arizona*-like "*I love him so mu-uu-uch!*" and said that yes, I feel like a completely different person now and my *lands*, the differences, they are many in number, although I can't really think of any right now beyond a heightened tolerance for another human being's bodily fluids.

Jason shrugged and said he didn't feel that different.

And I went all Precious-Moments eyeballs on him for a moment, because if he didn't feel different, that must mean he doesn't love Noah, because again, the multitude of differences! Like there are soggy burp cloths in my Coach bag! THAT'S A LIFE TURNED UPSIDE DOWN, I TELL YOU.

Jason tried to explain, ignoring my weirdness like he has ignored my weirdness for the past eight years, that while yes, our day-to-day lives are very different, he doesn't feel like he as a person has changed at all. Having Noah hasn't made him a better person who always gives change to homeless people or who has any deep insight into the human condition. It hasn't even changed how fast he drives.

And other than me still not being quite up to par in the seduction department, we as a couple haven't changed much either. We still talk about non-Noah things, like the pets and our jobs and people who bug us and, man, a vacation would be nice soon but, man, this thing at work, like, man, it's probably going to kill me dead. Please pour me another glass of wine. (Yes, we've always been this exciting. And eloquent!)

Jason summed up his feelings: now we have Noah. That in itself is huge. Noah is here and we need to take care of him, but taking care of him is fun and amazing, so therefore Noah makes our lives more fun and, wow, so glad we finally got knocked up and that we got knocked up with this particular little person. But being a dad is not the earth-shattering, ground-swelling, clouds-parting, surging-Bellagio-fountains kind of life change he thought it would be.

"Like when we got married," he said. "Everyone kept asking if I felt different. And I didn't. We were just married, and it was great, but not that different."

I responded by telling him that this was the craziest crazy talk I had ever heard, you big fat crazy, and spent the rest of our dinner contemplating my sleeping son, my incredibly delicious rockfish, and all the ways motherhood has changed me.

(Which I will now tell you about. Don't you like how I set that up? Respect the segue, people.)

Before Noah was born, people told me that having a child is like having your heart living outside of your body.

And I would nod because, yeah, I can totally see that. Their joy is your joy, their hurt is your hurt, blah blah weepcakes.

But then Noah was born, and this sentiment doesn't even come close.

My love for him is so visceral and deep that it's almost violent. It consumes me. It makes me want to swallow him whole. To put him back in my womb where he belonged exclusively to me, where I could keep him safe and secure.

Now that we have Noah, I feel like someone scraped off the top layer of my skin and created an entirely new little person with it.

I feel everything that he feels—every hug, kiss, and mean, old needle prick. And I'm standing over here with no skin at all—raw, exposed, and vulnerable.

I recently spent a weekend stomping around my house and threatening to pull down my whole damn stupid Web site because what am I *doing*, putting myself and my son out there so freaks and weirdos and mean people can be freaky and weird and mean to us. DO NOT FUCK WITH THE MAMA BEAR.

So that's a change. Probably not a good change. Probably a change I should discuss with my therapist, had I not fired my therapist because I cannot afford good emotional health right now, I have to buy diapers.

One thing my therapist *would* be proud of me for is my sort-of overcoming of the thing about the phone. (That's what we called it: The Thing About the Phone. Not strong enough to be considered a phobia [volcanoes!], but intrusive enough to be a definite Thing.)

I hate the phone. *Haaaate* it. I've hated it ever since I was in the first grade and could never remember my phone number. Every time I tried to call home from my friend Missy's house I dialed wrong, and one time this really mean lady yelled at me because she thought I was some punk kid when I just needed to ask my mom if I could stay for dinner. (And this *scarred me for life*. My neuroses are so fucking lame.) (And I didn't even *like* eating dinner at Missy's house, because her mom made canned green beans instead of frozen green beans and put onions *in* the hamburgers. So not worth a lifelong Thing, is all I'm saying.)

But Noah can't make his own pediatrician appointments, nor can he sweet talk his way to the top of daycare waiting lists, so I use the phone now.

I even called some random guy who left a Post-It on my car window asking where I'd gotten my leather interior done to tell him (we did it ourselves, and by "we" I mean "Jason") because it seemed like a nice, normal-phone-using thing to do. Also, I respect anyone who has a Post-It handy in a parking garage.

I still have not called to order Indian food though, because the woman who answers the phone at the restaurant is snippy, and snippy stills makes me nervous, and when I'm nervous I give them the wrong street address.

I feel bad about when I judged people for their screaming babies ("Just give the damn thing a pacifier already. All babies like pacifiers, right? *God*"), or for buying an SUV after having one child ("What, like you need all that room for a seven-pound infant? *God*"), or got angry because someone didn't call me or repeatedly canceled lunch plans while on maternity leave ("She's sitting at home eating bonbons in her jammies! She's totally going to spoil that damn baby and have no friends or life ever again and it'll be all her fault.") ("*God*.")

And I'm suddenly aware of money. Before Noah, we never worried about money. We never *thought* about money. If we ended up with some money for the savings account at the end of the month, that was *great*, but if not, *who cares*, look at the pretty things we bought! We'll think about retirement tomorrow or the day after that.

We're still doing just fine. We can pay our bills and have money left over, despite the insane amount of money I pay to Noah's day-care every month. Things are definitely tighter than before, but you know, the mortgage gets paid, and we can afford to go out for dinner. And after consulting our budget spreadsheet I have decided that I can, in fact, continue to pay twelve dollars a month for XM Radio because I no longer grocery shop while pregnant (i.e., seven pints of Ben & Jerry's, family-size tub of pudding, etc.).

But I'm just kind of obsessed with money anyway. I won't spend anything on myself, like *at all*. Every day at work, I scavenge around the kitchen and put together a free lunch of leftover lunch trays from meetings and free birthday cake and even some mysterious Jell-O snack cups that appeared the other morning. Today I used a Sharpie to color the heel of a shoe that Ceiba chewed all to hell, and I don't think you can notice at all, unless you look directly at it.

I went to buy cat food this weekend and pitched a damn fit because *my God*, did we not realize we were paying $22.45 for a case of canned light food versus $19.78 for this other brand? That's a cost savings of more than a whole *dollar* at *least*, don't make me do the math, but honestly, that's ridiculous of us to have never noticed that.

But I'm not forgoing simple pleasures like lunch and new shoes while lavishing hundreds of dollars on Noah either. I almost bought him generic formula on *principle*, but got scared of it, like what if it's the Hydrox equivalent to Oreos? Hydrox cookies are gross. And the generic diapers gave him a rash.

I've even been making homemade baby food. Not so I can ensure that he will only ever poop out the finest organic produce money can buy, but because those twee little jars are a rip-off.

(I'm sure many people out there are screaming WELCOME TO PLANET EARTH, BITCH right now. To them I say, THANK YOU. I ENJOY YOUR OXYGEN-RICH ATMOSPHERE AND VARIOUS CARBON-BASED LIFE FORMS. MAY I CLIP THAT COUPON FOR ALL-BEEF HOT DOGS IF YOU DO NOT PLAN TO UTILIZE IT FOR YOUR OWN NUCLEAR HOUSEHOLD?)

I am fairly sure, however, that my recent decent into miserhood is definitely temporary and will end sometime around the same time I run out of my good facial moisturizer.

I'm also trying to watch my language, *surprise, surprise*. I'm also having a tough time doing it, *duh, duh, duh, duh, DUH*. When I dropped the baby-food-making mixer attachment on my toe and broke the damn thing, I screamed the f-word several times, only to see Jason standing in the doorway, precious babe in arms. Later that night I broke a jar of red pepper flakes (from *Balducci's*, like, are we just throwing money out the window here?) and let a few more choice words fly.

The other night we realized that Noah was staring at the TV while a commercial for an ultraviolent horror movie was on. Jason casually turned him around and started talking to him *very loudly* while I fumbled for the remote.

But then yesterday I stumbled onto the Radio Disney channel on XM, only to hear them edit "piece of crap" out of a Weezer song. Seriously? Like, are you fucking kidding me?

And it threw me into an existential dilemma. We all want to be the cool parents who don't freak out about a bit of potty language and buy the stupid edited versions of CDs at Wal-Mart and whatever, but no one wants to be the parent of the kid who calls their preschool teacher a fucking douche.

Or even a piece of crap. Hmm.

So I guess I'm not really different either, except that I think about a lot of weird things now. Like when to learn how to use the parental controls on the TiVo. Or whether a subscription to the Sunday paper would be worth it for the coupons, and would I really remember to use the coupons, because who am I kidding?

I can tell you this much: parenthood is not sainthood. I am not a better person for fulfilling a base evolutionary urge to reproduce and pass on my clearly superior genetic code. Mostly I just feel like I'm just trying to not mess this kid up too badly.

If anything, being a parent just magnifies my insecurities and makes my bad habits more obvious. It would be really great if having a child automatically made me a kinder, gentler, more fiscally responsible, phone-using person who watches her goddamn motherfucking mouth sometimes. I guess I thought it would, and I'm sometimes a little thrown to realize I'm just as flawed as ever.

I guess the only real life-changing difference is this: now we have Noah.

BE CAREFUL WHAT YOU WISH FOR

Susan Wagner FRIDAY PLAYDATE

I am fascinated by the current Build a Smarter Baby Brain trend, by the lengths to which parents feel compelled to go to give their progeny an edge. Frankly, this idea that there's only one thing better than having a baby, and that's having a smart baby, makes me almost unbearably sad. I *have* a smart baby—I have two, actually, but one is, I think, the ubersmart baby that these parents are hoping for, striving for. And I want to say to them: be careful what you wish for.

Henry tests in the ninety-ninth percentile for verbal ability; he knows more words than most children his age and can use them to form grammatically complex sentences and paragraphs. His rote memory is off the charts. The doctor who tested him said, "It was amazing! I kept doing the test because I couldn't believe how much and how perfectly he could remember!" Yes, we said, we know. When he comes across a new word, he will ask us to define it, to use it in a sentence, and often to spell it for him. He will incorporate it into conversation.

One day last year, he went to school in a Spider-Man T-shirt. Another boy in his class had on a different Spider-Man T-shirt. Henry told his teacher, "Jack's shirt has a picture of Spider-Man, but my shirt just has his logo." He was right, but how many four-year-olds know what a logo is? Henry does, because he had been asking about the picture on my Starbucks coffee cup, and I told him, "That's their corporate logo."

Admit it, some of you are envious. You want to know what we did to build his vocabulary, how we taught him to contextualize and utilize all those words. It had to be more than just a casual conversation about the picture on my take-out coffee cup! Flash cards? Computer games? Tutoring? Wait, just wait.

Rote memory: Henry remembers everything. He can recite dialogue from movies, accurately, with proper inflection and, often, accent. He can recite entire picture books. He has memorized large sections of the Winnie the Pooh stories. He knows the words to every song on *In My Tribe* by 10,000 Maniacs. When he cannot hear clearly what the words are, he asks. And then he remembers them. He will sometimes sing "Hey Jack Kerouac" in the bathtub. He has excellent pitch, too, and a nice singing voice.

Again, you are thinking, how did we do that? What is the secret? Because, my God! How wonderful to have such a *smart* baby! He will certainly do well! Be successful! Make you proud!

But what you don't see is this: Henry has been diagnosed with nonverbal learning disability. His verbal aptitude is remarkable, but his pragmatic language skills—his ability to understand tone of voice or facial gestures or even the simple conventions of conversation—are simply average. He can wax eloquent about *Harry Potter and the Sorcerer's Stone*, recounting the events of the plot in great and accurate detail, but he cannot tell you why Harry and Ron would take on a mountain troll to save Hermione, or why Ron would sacrifice himself in the chess game, or why the touch of Harry's hand is fatal to Professor Quirrell. He does not understand how language is used to construct relationships; he cannot infer when someone is angry or amused or embarrassed. Because of this, he struggles with basic social interactions. He becomes frustrated, this overly verbal child, to the point of catastrophic tantrums when other people can't understand what he is talking about or don't share his interests.

"Why doesn't Luke like superheroes?" he asked me this summer.

"He just doesn't," I said.

"But *I* do!" he said, clearly baffled. "And Luke is my best friend!"

"OK," I told him, "but Luke likes turkey sandwichs. Do you like turkey?'"

"No," he said. "You know I don't like turkey."

"Well," I said, "different people like different things."

He thought about this. "But why doesn't Luke like superheroes?" he asked again. And we went on and on like this, all summer, until Luke finally decided to like superheroes. Henry couldn't understand how Luke, who is his *best friend*, could not like what he did.

When we tell people about Henry's disability, the first thing they say is, "But he's so *smart!*" They talk about his verbal skills. One friend said, "But he will do fine in school, won't he? How can he not? He's so smart!" The answer is that he will and he won't. Math may be a struggle for him, especially word problems. He will have trouble gleaning the meaning of what he reads, despite his ability to memorize the actual text. He will struggle with social skills. He may be teased. With tutoring and therapy, in the right school, he will do fine. But it will not be easy, even though he is so smart.

I read about parents buying computers for their babies, hoping to give them a head start, to teach them letters and numbers and reading and counting before all the baby books say they should be doing those things. I have a friend whose son, on his own, was reading before he was two. I remember feeling envious when, at two,

Henry was barely talking. But my friend's son was subsequently diagnosed with Asperger's Syndrome (one characteristic of which is hyperlexia, or early reading). I sometimes wonder, when I take Henry to story time or out for coffee or other places where people see him and hear him talking with me, in his very sophisticated and grown-up way, and comment on how smart he is and how they wish their child spoke like that, knew all those words, I sometimes wonder if those parents have any idea what it means to have a child who is gifted, who is, truly, so very smart. If they have any idea that this smartness is a complicated gift, or that the real gift is to have a child who is healthy and happy and who knows that he is loved unconditionally.

We did not do anything special with Henry—no flash cards, no computer software, no tutoring. This is just the way his brain works. What I want to say to the mother who wants the smart baby is this: Enjoy the way your child's brain works. Play with her, talk to her, value who she is. Don't try to reprogram her. Just love her.

THE MOST HANDSOMEST

Miriam Kamin WOULDA COULDA SHOULDA

Everything I ever need to know about good self-esteem I learned from my son.

Today Monkey is having his class pictures taken. Last night, I asked him if he wanted to help me pick out what he would wear. He's coming up on five now, you know, so I figured he might want to have a say. Little did I know.

"Let's try on this shirt," I said brightly. He eyed it and then slipped his arms in. It was too big, because you don't actually grow all that fast on the all Pop-Tart diet. "OK, not this one. Take it off, please. How about this red one?" That one fit, and he spun around for me to admire him.

"This one is very handsome," he told me. "Do you think I should maybe wear a tie?" I raised my eyebrows. He pointed back into the closet. "There's a tie hanging on that hanger. I think it would make me even *more* handsome." I bit my lip to keep from laughing and brought the tie out for his inspection. "Oh, diggers and trucks! This is *perfect*!" he exclaimed.

I couldn't resist giving him a squeeze as I laid the shirt and tie out on his chair. "Okay, honey, go brush your teeth, please."

"Okay, Mama." He trotted out to the bathroom and then spun around and came back, a single finger perched in the air to signal a matter of great importance. "Um, Mama?"

"Yes, love?"

"Which pants will I be wearing?" I choked just a little, but managed to keep a serious face.

"These jeans, I think," I said, showing him the jeans I'd taken out before we picked the shirt. He tilted his head at his dungarees and shook it ever so slightly.

"Mama, don't you think I would be even more handsomer in some nicer pants with my red shirt and my tie?"

"Oh!" Clearly I hadn't realized the can of worms I'd opened. "Well, maybe you're right. Shall I pull out a pair of church pants, do you think?"

"Yes, please." He watched me like a hawk while I dug through his pants drawer and pulled out a pair of cuffed khaki chinos.

"Do you think these are OK?"

"Yes, those will be lovely." I swear to God I am not making this up. If you have never seen a small boy declare his pants lovely, you simply have not lived. "Um, Mama?"

"Yes?"

"Do those pants have the, uh," he was gesticulating wildly, and I waited. "The um, thingies that are for trapping a belt?"

"Oh! Belt loops?" He brightened.

"Yes! Belt loopses! Does it have those?"

"Yes, these pants have belt loops. Do you suppose you need a belt, as well?"

"*Mama*," now the rolling of eyes; yes! Clearly I am so brain damaged my ability just to breathe with regularity is astonishing. "Of *course* I need a belt to look handsomest!"

"OK, that's fine, I'll take out your belt, too. Anything else?" He pondered for a moment.

"Nice shoes?"

"They're downstairs in the mudroom. I think you're all set, buddy."

"OK. You are going to be buying lots of my pictures, because I am going to be so handsome you can't stand it, I think."

At this point, I *had* to laugh, because it was a necessary release to prevent the melting of my brain and heart from excessive adorableness. "I think you are exactly right, Monkey."

Fast-forward to this morning. Breakfast was peppered with practice smiles and running commentary on how he would not paint today, and he would be very careful not to get dirty, and he wondered if any of his friends would be nearly so handsome as he. (Probably not, we concluded.) Chickadee doesn't have photos until the next week, so she ate in sullen silence and whispered to Monkey that his tie was stupid when she thought I wasn't listening. This didn't produce even the slightest damper on his mood of self-adoration, thankfully.

We arrived at the bus stop and Monkey went to each of the three neighbor girls, in turn, to announce, "I am wearing a tie today. Because I am handsome." He took their giggling for agreement, and threw his arms around my legs as the bus arrived. "Bye, Chickie!" he called out. Then, "Mama, I am so excited to be so handsomish for pictures. Let's get me to school!"

I brushed his hair one last time and gave him a kiss as he ran off to show his tie to his friends. "Oh, Monkey, don't you look handsome!" gushed one of the teachers.

"Yes!" he agreed. I should be embarrassed, I guess. But why? He's very matter-of-fact about his elite status. His joy is contagious. He is, after all, the most handsomest. We should all be so kind to ourselves.

A CHINK IN THE ARMOR
Jenny Lauck THREE KID CIRCUS

Yesterday, my three-year-old and I watched some music videos. One of the songs featured a child dressed in a robot costume made from a foil-covered box.

My girl turned to me and with stiff arms moving in jerky, up-and-down motions, said in a monotone, "Hello. Robot. Mommy."

I answered her, doing my best Mr. Roboto. "Domo. Arigato."

She didn't break character for a second. "My. Name. Is. Baby. Robot. You. Are. Mommy. Robot. I. Need. A. Box. Costume."

Ha! Lucky for her, I had a small cardboard box, just perfect for a pint-sized robot. I cut out a hole for her head and two holes for her arms. She beamed at me and then proceeded to march stiff-legged, with arms bent at the elbow and occasionally chopping through the air. "I. Need. A. Juice. Box," she announced. "I. Need. Some. Fuel."

My oldest daughter got in on the act, and I made her a cardboard costume as well.

My son decided from the moment he came upon us that we were all a bunch of dorks, and he didn't want to join in our game. This is the boy who *laller laller laller lallers* and flaps his hands and makes high-pitched "meep" noises and is generally annoying, just because.

"What. Is. The. Matter. Robot. Boy?" He was annoyed. I needled him for a bit longer, but ultimately decided to go make dinner. I told the girls to back off, but secretly laughed while they continued to speak to him in Robot. Language.

He fled to his room with the robot sisters in hot pursuit. What came next was a scream that to this day makes the hair on the back of my neck stand up, just thinking about it. A high-pitched wail of pain that just went on and on.

I raced back to the bedroom. My two daughters stood looking concerned. My son, already on his feet and looking green, had a huge scrape down the length of his face. He had fallen forward off his bunk bed ladder and taken the full impact with a nearby book-shelf with his jaw.

Mentally, I felt myself slip into an insulated, calm space. I casually carried him to the couch, got ice, administered painkillers, talked to my husband, checked inside of my son's mouth for any cuts, and finally carried him to the van for the fifteen-minute drive to the emergency room.

After the impact he was dizzy and nauseous, and although his pupils were fine I was scared. When the first rush of the trauma wore off, he began to cry softly, and kept asking to sleep. *Crap, crap, crap.*

Still calm, I registered with the ER check-in and sat down, talking to him about school, asking about toys. He stopped crying. By the time we spoke to the triage nurse, he was answering all the questions and arguing with me. We returned to the waiting room. After a few minutes, he was called back and examined by a doctor.

She pronounced him a very lucky boy and warned him about playing on the bunk bed. Aside from two very nasty scrapes and some swelling, he's fine. He's totally fine.

We returned home to my pale and worried husband and reported the good news. We tucked the kids into bed and went to sleep ourselves. The next morning, we got up and got out of the house. I did some shopping, and when I got back in the van to come home I just lost it. I sat in the Target parking lot and shook like a leaf, crying.

I don't think I realized how scared I was last night, and I never let myself go there. Even after we were all safe in bed, I thought, "Whew!" and drifted off to sleep. Today, however, the what-ifs are hanging like a cloud over me.

I've dried my tears, and I'm putting one foot in front of the other. It feels like I've been handed a giant warning notice from the parenting gods, and at the same time, a giant "get out of jail free" card. We are so lucky.

We are so lucky.

CORN ON THE CAM

Birdie Jaworksi BIRDIE JAWORSKI

Ever since my two young boys discovered wormholes and shape-shifting aliens, I promised we would visit the Star Trek Experience in America's city of sin. I put the trip off for months, then a year. Las Vegas ain't cheap, and the Hilton charges a cool forty dollars a warm body to hurl through space and time in a jolting metal chair surrounded by 3-D images and two-bit actors. But a promise is a promise. I hoarded my money and served black beans and rice for six weeks until I saved exactly enough to treat two Trekkies to an overnight trip.

"We still have to be careful," I told the boys as I stuffed a paper bag with bread and bananas and a package of pretzels. "Since I'm going to spend a bunch of money in Las Vegas, we're going to eat peanut butter sandwiches along the way. No stopping for snacks, OK? We'll leave at the crack of dawn."

My youngest son, 8, ran to his bedroom. I heard him unzip his backpack, heard the clatter and clang of a million handheld star-ships against canvas and zipper. His older brother, 10, stared into the space above my head, as if some travel angel whispered advice.

"Uh, Mom?" He stuck his hands behind his back and tipped his body up on sandaled heels. "Doesn't it take, like, all day to get to Las Vegas? Why don't you use that car cookbook?"

Car cookbook? It took a moment, but then I remembered a Saturday morning yard sale in a tired inland neighborhood, a slim worn paperback called *Manifold Destiny*, and a bored woman wearing denim overalls and scuffed army boots who accepted my offer of ten cents.

"I'll go get it, Mom. It's under my bed." 10 ran to retrieve the book, and I shook my head. Weird kid.

10 read the book out loud as I handed the scraggly-haired neighbor girl twenty dollars and a list of pet-care instructions.

"Mom, we need aluminum foil. The recipes tell you to wrap your food in foil and then stick it next to the hottest part of the engine. Is our car more like a Lamborghini or a BMW?" I glanced over his shoulder and read the funny captions comparing the cooking abilities of fancy cars. I pictured our sensible family vehicle, the way it smelled of dog hair and spilled bubble bath.

"Lamborghini. Definitely." I rolled my eyes and told 10 to choose a few engine recipes and to pack the ingredients. "You're in charge."

The next morning I hauled the boys' backpacks to the car while 10 prepared the first of our engine delights. He balanced three wrapped packages in the crook of one arm and carried our small, red cooler in the other. He waited while I lifted the hood and placed the foil packets gently here and there, next to places that would glow with invisible heat as we crossed the lichen-studded Mojave desert. His face looked studious, artful, as if he were a traveling four-star chef, and I noticed how elegantly each square serving was folded, an origami feast. I slammed down the hood.

"Wow, you really did a nice job. So, what's for breakfast?" I rubbed his dark hair.

10 waved his arms over the car in some kind of magician's swirl. "Our first course is grilled cheese. The book says to cook them for fifty-five miles."

8 piled into the backseat holding two Star Trek action figures, a box of colored pencils, and a stack of drawing paper. "Rats. I wanted French toast."

Las Vegas was six hours away, but with two young boys and a rolling cookout I knew the road would stretch four hours longer, feel like ten days later, hurt like five years older, with tired legs and red-rimmed eyes at the end. We turned north, then east, and 10 watched the odometer with hawk eyes and nervous fingers, the road-grill bible in his lap.

Mile fifty-five meant grilled cheese breakfast, and we pulled over one mile early at a rest stop outside of Los Angeles to steaming squares of soft bread filled with melted swiss. The California border town of Blythe meant a snack of s'mores, consisting of graham crackers filled with oozing chocolate and marshmallows, all wrapped in the ubiquitous tin foil, eaten along I-15 in the red brick of mid morning, the dry heat of August sand stinging our eyes and hands, matching degree for degree the heat of our campfire car snack. The thermometer reached ninety, then ninety-nine, one-hundred, one-hundred-three, then leveled out at one-hundred-thirteen as we hit the plane of the Mojave near midday.

10 fussed, his hands in the cooler, the backseat beginning to drip from ice-cube condensation. 8 slept soundly, Wesley Crusher and Lt. Worf in his hands, tiny pieces of foil littering the back seat. I glanced in the rearview mirror, watched 10 place three pieces of foil per serving in his lap. He held the book in one hand, his other sprinkling pieces of chopped potato onto the silver sheets. He brought

cut potatoes? I tried to think of when he might have prepared the ingredients, but drew a blank. He sprinkled salt from my good ceramic shaker—the one Gramma left me—and I bit my tongue, not wanting to erase his enthusiasm, his scientific excitement. He balanced the shaker on the arm rest, and I took three deep breaths, swung the car into an exit lane, and pulled into an ancient forgotten riverbed to pop the hood. 10 pulled on my gardening gloves and opened the side door. A blast of mercury heat filled the car, swelling my hands as 10 stuffed packets of potatoes and green beans into the nooks and crannies of our engine.

The car shot like a green light against the highway, and our countenance sifting along the sands like pathetic flotsam caught the attention of six dudes on Harleys that I saw pull up behind us, a swarm of chain-link, midday ghosts.

"Hey! Get back in the car this instant!" I screamed out the window at 10 as the bikers ground to a stop, a splinter spray of tumbleweed and pea gravel behind them. My son left the hood open, and I watched dust swirl around us, into the engine, coating the little silver lunches with ancient ocean dust. I locked the doors.

The bikers lifted helmets from heads, left legs supporting machines, a row of black, studded dominoes one right after the other, and the man closest to our car lifted right leg over engine as he strode quickly to my window. I pressed the button to lower it one inch.

"Everything OK, Miss?" His face was red-brown from a thousand desert drives, and tiny beads of sweat collected around the black hair pulled back from his face into a short ponytail. He kept his hands at his hips, fingers splayed across the edges of his leather chaps. I tried not to stare at the extra pinky on his left hand. The strains of Fleetwood Mac blared from the radio, and I reached to quiet it.

"Yes, thank you, but we're doing great. Just taking a break. Thanks for stopping and asking. Have a great ride!" I spoke fast. My words shot out the window, bounced off his leather vest and into the dirt between his boots. In the rearview mirror, I saw three of the other bikers swarm around my car, making a beeline for the open hood.

"Hey! Don't touch our lunch!" 10 rolled down his window and stuck his head out the window. "I spent eighteen miles making that lunch!"

The bikers turned and stared at 10's coarse dark hair standing at Kewpie-doll attention in the Mojave wind.

"You're cooking, son?" A tall biker in worn black leather strode to 10's window. "What's for lunch?"

He looked just a bit older than me, but sandblasted, as if his clothes and skin and dirt-swept hair rose from the Palo Verde roots beneath us, and grew a man tree with legs like leather-clad trunks and arms carved with initials twisted in muscle. I held my breath, ready to gun the engine, hood up and visibility at zero, to do what I needed to do to protect my family.

"I've been slaving over a hot engine all day." 10 smirked and waited for laughter that didn't come. The biker's eyes faded a bit, tried to make sense of 10's banter. "For lunch, I am making roasted potatoes and corn and warming up left-over pizza. My mom got this book at a yard sale, and I am just following the instructions." He held the book up, carefully, reverentially, then slowly turned it side to side, front to back. The biker nodded his head. A lock of hair with natural highlights fell into his right eye.

As 10 explained, the rest of the men gathered close to the engine, lifting and examining the foil squares.

"Excuse me, boy. Did you add any herbs to the potatoes? Rosemary? Olive oil?" A burly man in a vintage AC/DC long-sleeved T-shirt leaned to the left of the hood and rubbed his full beard with one hand. "Sliced or cut?" His belly hung over the silver skull-and-crossbones buckle set below his waist. "Got any more of that foil?"

My son reached below his seat and pulled out the cardboard box housing the wrap. "How much do you want?" He yelled outside, but the wind carried his words in the opposite direction.

What the hell, I thought. Culinary bikers can't be all that bad. "OK, guys, we can get outside and check on the lunch."

10 passed around pieces of foil while the bikers opened pannier bags and coolers and found bits and pieces of food for their own cookout.

"Am I doing this right?" A man with a fringed jacket and a snake tattoo slithering along his neck stuffed a foil-wrapped sandwich in the cylinder-head cleavage of his bike. "How many miles do you think?" 10 walked to the bike with book in hand and gave it the once-over.

"Looks good. I'd give it forty-five miles. But not a mile more!"

The bikers and their roasting dinners peeled back onto the highway, and we hit the road too, drove slow and easy as the sun moved from noon to the high heat of early afternoon. We stopped again to retrieve our finished potatoes, corn, and pizza along the shoulder of old Route 66. An elderly couple saw our raised hood and pulled behind us. I walked to greet them at their car door, foil packet in hand.

"Hello! Thanks for stopping, but we're not in car trouble. We're just cooking lunch. Here, I am offering all good Samaritans samples of pizza, corn on the cob, and roasted potatoes." I held out a box of plastic forks and an unopened lunch packet. The woman held her husband's arm, kept him from accepting our bounty. A transparent blue scarf held her up-do in place. "Don't you people have a stove at home?"

A few hours and two more meals later, the engine started smelling like Gramma's house three days past Thanksgiving, an unforgiving odor of overheated oils and cheeses and meats and burnt vegetables.

"Mooooooooom, I think that smell's gonna make me barf." 8 curled next to his open window, holding his nose with forefinger and thumb.

What to do? I stopped the car for fuel and opened the hood, tried to find bits and pieces of leftovers that might contribute to any smell, but the cavity was relatively clean. I opened my purse, hoping to find a sample bottle of fragrance to mask the smell inside the car, but the only thing I could find was a tube of bubblegum flavored lip balm. I opened the cap, twisted it, let it slide along my top and bottom lip, passed it to 10 and 8 to do the same. "Here, use this while I've got it. Our lips will chap in this desert heat."

And then I did something that I wasn't sure was good for the engine. I ran the lip balm along the engine, let it melt into a fine layer. As we drove into the red-flash city of greed, our noses met the sweet scent of overheated bubblegum.

I shook the boys awake, and they dragged backpacks and action figures into the smoke-filled lobby of the Hilton casino hotel. The clerk handed me a room key and brochures detailing the sights and sounds of Las Vegas. She chomped grape-flavored gum, and as she breathed I smelled all of her unheard hopes inside a cloud of cigarettes and artificial flavor.

"Welcome to Las Vegas. Enjoy your stay. Oh! And you came all the way from San Diego! You must be hungry after all that road food. Here are some coupons for discounts at our twenty-four-hour buffet. I bet those growing boys are hungry!"

I saw 10 reach into his backpack for his road-grill bible. The slot machines chimed and cursed behind us. I grabbed the key and coupons and gave the kids The Look that meant Shut Up and Let's Get the Hell Outta Here, and I pushed them toward the elevator.

As I used all my mom's strength to get the boys' attention toward bed and away from the spinning lights, I heard 10 yell back toward the lobby desk.

"Ma'am! Road food can be sublime!"

·

9

Personal Growth Blows

When my daughter was born, my father-in-law, patriarch of eight children, told me, "The hardest part about being a parent is having to give up what you really want to do." I thought he meant going to bars, staying up late, and eating cereal for dinner.

As my daughter got older, I realized what he meant was bigger than that. He meant having to give up, put off, or squeeze into the wee hours my writing. He meant having to take jobs that could provide health insurance. He meant choosing between private school and staying in our beautiful, old house in the city or living in the suburbs with a great, free school district. He meant missing the fireworks on the Fourth of July because the baby was sleeping. He meant not having time to work on my marriage right when it needed the work.

He meant learning to use my free time for things that needed to be done, not things I wanted to do.

I didn't get pregnant until I was twenty-nine. I know many women, some of them contributors to this book, who are having babies well into their late thirties and beyond. We spent years indulging our own preferences only to have to learn in the course of twenty-four hours, some of which may have been spent screaming in pain, how to put another human being's needs and development first. I'm not going to lie to you, it's hard. Really hard.

There is a bright side, though—growth. Becoming a parent teaches you who you are and helps you to correct character flaws you didn't even realize you had. Teaching a little person how the world works inserts "please" back into your language, forces you to call your mother more often, and insists you confront your personal demons before they are passed along. Personal growth hurts, but you emerge a better human being.

YOU CAN NEVER OUT-LOVE
YOUR MOM

Jennifer Satterwhite MOMMY NEEDS COFFEE

Since becoming a mother, I have discovered something that I never imagined to be true when I was growing up, something my mother used to say to me, but I always told her it was impossible. Turns out, she was right. She always told me you can never out-love your mother. And you can't. It is impossible. Even when she is your hero, as my mom has always been to me.

I am a mother to three and know that there is no way they could ever love me more than I love them. There is no way will they know the deep intensity of love for the very beings that I brought into this world and am raising to one day go forward and change the world around them. They could never out-love me.

Just as I can never out-love my own mom.

As a little girl, I learned more from Mom than I could ever document in an essay or column. I learned how to be the woman I am today. I probably even learned my disdain for sorting socks from her. The best thing I learned from her was to laugh. You just have to laugh in the face of any horror you are confronted with. You have to look at fear, pain, and, yes, even death, and laugh—or you will cry, and it will win. What an amazing gift she gave me with her laughter and her humor.

I was always Mommy's Little Helper growing up. Perhaps it was the youngest child syndrome, or maybe the suck-up gene. But honestly, I think it had more to do with the fact that I thoroughly enjoyed her company. She made anything and everything fun. Nothing was so bad that she couldn't find either humor in it or a way to remind you why you should be laughing. Helping her out was my greatest joy as a little girl. I would "help" her fold clothes. (Which probably always led to her redoing them later, but never in front of me.) I would "help" her clean the dishes. (Which equated to making lots of bubbles and getting the sink, floor, and both of us soaking wet.) I would "help" her carry heavy things that looked like they were too much for her to carry alone. (Now I see that she was carrying it and I was merely placing my hands on it, probably making it heavier.) It is now that I have my own Mommy's Little Helper that I realize how little I was helping her and how much she was actually helping me. A mother's love. There is nothing like it.

And no pain like knowing it is going to leave your life.

There is a certain grief that comes before death. A cruel time of waiting. A limbo during which you desperately want more time, yet agonize over every new ailment or setback. A time when you desperately want death to just *hurry up* if it is going to come. Just *stop* taking her piece by piece. Stop robbing us of her bit by bit until she is no longer there. There is a cruelty to a slow death that torments those who are standing on the sidelines watching it happen, for those of us who see it lurking in the corner and wonder, "Are you coming? Is it time? What do we do until you decide to stop this sadistic dance and let the music finally end?"

Honestly, I get really mad at all of this. I want to scream at Death and tell it to just stop screwing around with her. To just go away until it is time. But it hasn't listened. It sneaks in, steals another part of Mom, and slithers back out. To those who haven't known her forever, it is hardly noticeable when she has been robbed of another aspect of what makes her who she is. To those of us who have always known her, there is a huge emptiness left behind. A hole in the very essence of who she is that has been taken from us, before we were ready.

I can't stop what is happening to her. I can't do anything to ease it or make it less cruel. I can't even be there for her on a daily basis. There are days I am so thankful that I don't have to face this in person on a day-to-day basis. And then I hate myself for thinking that. For being thankful that I don't have to watch her go. How awful is it that I find relief in my absence? Because when I am with her, I hurt. Because there is still so much I have to say to her. There is so much that I need to know. Why didn't I ask her about the little things when there was time? Why didn't I tell her that being her daughter was the most fun, most amazing experience in the world? Why didn't I ask her to share more of her stories with me? And then the anger hits again.

The last time I was with her, she apologized. Can you believe that? She apologized to me that she was so sick. She cannot even use her voice past her trache tube, yet she managed to whisper out the very words I have been telling her. I'm so sorry.

I hope I have told her enough that she was a good mom. I hope I have given her enough love to get her through those hard times in our past of slammed doors and rolled eyes. I hope she knows that although I am aware I can never out-love my mom, I sure can come close.

It has been a few days since she has been awake when she has visitors. The doctors refer to her as minimally responsive, which basically means if you poke her with a needle or start a procedure on her, she will open her eyes wide and give you a scared look, followed by a "go to hell" look. But when my dad has been there, she wouldn't wake up to see him. When my sister was there, Mom opened her eyes once after my sister repeatedly and loudly told her to open her eyes. Very loudly and very sternly, as Mom must have done for us as children when we were not responding to her when she was asking us to do something for her.

My heart shatters each time I hear that she is asleep more than awake now. Does she know what is happening? Is she scared? Does she wonder why I am not sitting by her bedside holding her hand as she has done for me countless times? Or has Death done its only merciful act and already stolen her ability to reason those things out?

Bit by bit. Day by day. I grieve for her. In a way, I wonder if these little deaths are more painful than the big one that is inevitable. There is a desperation that wants this nightmare to end, yet a fear that never wants her to leave me, because I love her and cannot imagine her not being here. And this waiting, this watching, this grieving, it is hard. I wonder what she must be thinking when I stand beside her bed and tell her how much I love her. I wonder if she hears me and knows all of the things I want to say but just cannot find the words for. Yet, when I leave her and return home to my boys and my own baby girl and hold them in my arms or watch them play, or even when I stand over their sleeping bodies when I check on them at night, I am comforted in knowing that no matter how much I love Mom, there is a peace that comes and surrounds me just by knowing this very basic truth.

You can never out-love your mom.

My mother passed away peacefully on January 6, 2006. Each day I am with my children, I am reminded of the intense love she gave me, and I pray that each day I can show my children the love and devotion she gave me. I owe her at least that much.

NICOLE RICHIE HAS NOTHING ON ME

Rita Arens SURRENDER, DOROTHY

I spent this weekend with two dear college roommates and their families. A good time was had by all, with four children, five adults, and one very sweet and old yellow lab that I remember Kristin getting when the dog was just a wee puppy and the girl lived with me on Church Street in Iowa City.

How time flies.

So there we were, cradling babies and startling toddlers awake when my beloved would bellow profanities at the football game on television. Kristin's parents often offer up their gorgeous and enormous house when we all come to visit, since our burgeoning group keeps getting bigger, with Cindy now pregnant again and Steph with a new beau and Nicole living with some fellow in D.C. that she never brings around and blah, blah, blah.

I sat there thinking about how far I have come in the past eleven years since I graduated from college and left behind (mostly) my eating disorder.

Ironically, Kristin brought home this week's *People* magazine, which boasted a cover screaming of celebrity skinniness. The picture of a skeletal Nicole Richie running on the beach brought up bile in my throat, because she looked so much like me at age eighteen, when I consumed five to seven hundred calories a day and vomited with the bathwater running on a regular basis.

I've blocked out a lot of that time, but I still remember making lists of the calories I ate that day in the margins of my college textbooks. I counted gum. I counted alcohol—probably why to this day I've never consumed a beer. I never developed a taste for it when most people were choking down Natty Light for a cheap buzz in dilapidated, rented-out houses. When I pledged my sorority in 1992, I wore a size two red dress. I now wear an eight or ten, depending on the season. At the time, I was thirty-five pounds lighter than I am now. I am in the middle of my appropriate body mass index now. And yet, I never dipped below 105 pounds, and that was my ticket to assuring most people that I was still "normal," even though I'm five foot six. Even at my lightest, I was still dense.

Despite the numbers not being that scary, my bones were horrifying. I would trace my fingers over my ribs every night to be sure I could still feel each one. I could feel my heart beating through my ribcage. Sometimes that scared me. A heavy door was hard to open, even though I exercised an hour and a half every day, seven days a week, including weekends and national holidays. Even when I was sick.

I started smoking my senior year of high school, a year after I started dieting. By the time I hit the University of Iowa, I was smoking a pack to a pack and a half a day, a habit I kept up until age twenty-five. Since then, it's been spotty. Most of the time, I'm "good," but every now and then I hear that old voice criticizing my inner thighs, and light up I do. Even as a mother. God, I hate myself when I do that.

My head was too big for my body. I could make my fingers into a circle and fit them around the very top of my thigh. When I tried to

•

go parasailing on vacation in Florida when I was eighteen, the parasail guy looked at my parents and told them he was afraid the rope might snap and whisk me away forever.

My sister, my parents, and my hometown friends were beside themselves, and they were sick of telling me I was going to die. Despite the fact that they stuck with me, they must've wanted to shoot me if I weren't already on the fast track to a heart attack. I was a pain. I denied my problems. I told them there was nothing wrong. I told them it was my life. I hated them for getting in my business, for caring about me when I was so hell-bent on hurting myself.

I did go to college, though, and I did make friends. The summer after my freshman year, I went home. When I came back that fall, I was about ten pounds heavier. When I came back for our sorority's first fall meeting, two of my friends started crying. My friend Julia told me she'd been certain I would die over the summer and she'd never see me again.

I don't really remember how I got better, I just know it wasn't an overnight process, and I never got professional help at the time. I started off a vegan, mostly to avoid eating anything with any real calories. I was eating cheese and eggs again by the time I was a college senior. I incorporated fish after I graduated, and I added back in poultry and pork after I married my beloved. At Cindy's house last year, I ate a hamburger, and everyone freaked out. It was the first time they'd seen me eat beef in fourteen years. I kind of had a tummy ache afterward, but it was good to be normal.

Getting pregnant was my own personal hell. As someone who's a control freak about my body and particularly my weight, it was worse than waterboarding to have to gain weight on purpose, without checking it and without knowing when it would stop. To boot,

I gained a ton of water weight—eight pounds of it my last week of pregnancy—and could leave lasting finger imprints on my legs at any time after six months. The scale was agony, and only knowing how badly it would hurt the little angel kept me from Just. Dieting. Anyway.

Pregnancy forced me to gain weight for someone else. And I hated every minute of it. However, the irony of the situation is that pregnancy seemed to reset my ailing metabolism—the same metabolism that had me gaining five pounds after one week of eating twelve hundred calories a day. Message to any ana-fans out there: be prepared to either die or fuck up your metabolism for years. *Years,* ladies. Yes, your ridiculous, low-calorie dieting will actually reset your metabolism at eight hundred calories a day, so if you try to recover you will gain weight faster than you want. Faster than you know how to accept. This message is not *keep dieting.* This message is *don't go low-cal in the first place.* I was lucky. Pregnancy fixed my body. After the little angel was born, I went back to my prepregnancy weight in four months, and dropped five pounds below that after she started crawling. I've since gained back the bonus five, but I never became the dumpy person I was so fucking afraid of becoming.

Eating disorders are selfish, and that's why it's so hard for people to be understanding. Outwardly, it seems the afflicted person is just being vain to the point of killing themselves. I'm here to tell you that's not the way it works. Eating disorders, textbook ones like the one I had, stem from the inability to control one's life. In my case, it stemmed from two bouts of maternal cancer at a formative age, mixed with a super-Type-A personality, and shot through with an inherited predisposition toward the melancholy. Sometimes there may seem to be no trigger point, but I guarantee that somewhere in that girl or woman's past (and it usually is a female) there was a combination of bad circumstance, perfectionism, and a mean comment about the girl's butt.

I grew up tormented by skinny people. I was not a skinny person. Looking back at photos, I was not as fat as I thought, but I never was a skinny kid in an age when most kids were skinny. It wasn't like now. People were wearing kids' 6X into middle school when I was a kid. A lot of comments got through to me. Wearing a leotard in dance class drove home how different I was from the others— something I worry about sometimes at my daughter's ballet classes. I have to remind myself that the little angel is not me and may not be plagued by my own insecurities.

I try so hard not to ever criticize my appearance in front of the little angel. I don't want her growing up with a complex. But my own mother was a skinny bird—she never said things like "I feel fat" when I was growing up, so I most certainly didn't get it from her. I want the little angel to always feel she is beautiful, but I'm a woman, too, and I'm just not naive enough to think she will understand how beautiful she is as a teenager. I am terrified she will doubt herself the way I have doubted myself. I want her to skip the journey and emerge on the other side.

My sister struggled with having red hair, because it made her different. I worry about that, too, since the little angel's shade is the exact same as the one I envied my entire childhood. So far, the little angel seems to be a beautiful child, and I do think she will grow into a beautiful young woman. She will probably go through a chubby stage—I did and my beloved did. I hope that I can give her the right message when she does. The message that yes, there is an awkward phase, but no, it will not last forever. I don't think lying to your kid does any good. My own mother said so many times that I wasn't fat that I wanted to beat her with a wet noodle. I almost would have felt better if she would've just said, "Yeah, you've got a little extra. So do I—let's go for a walk and skip the ice cream tonight." I have no idea how to talk about this with the little angel when she gets to that age. I don't know if it would be better to be honest about my mistakes or hold them back for fear of her repeating them.

I wish I had just been normal, so I wouldn't have to make these decisions.

A friend of mine commented some months ago that I seem to have a lot of body confidence. Most of the time (when my jeans fit), I do. Somewhere along the line, I learned to put more stock in the quality of my words and my friendships and relationships than I do my jeans size. I'm not completely cured, though. I don't think I'll ever fall into the abyss again, but the first thing in my mind when life is completely out of my control is that maybe dropping five might make me feel better. I'm sure I've got it under control now, fourteen years later, but that pain lurks somewhere in the depths of my personality.

That ability to blindly, fervently hate yourself.

I hope to God she never feels that way. I love her so much, and I can't stand the thought of her hating herself.

I finally understand how much my eating disorder must have hurt my mother.

I'm so sorry.

BAKE ME A CAKE

Risa Green MOMMY TRACK'D

First of all, not only do I not bake, I also don't cook, unless you count tossing some frozen things that are allegedly made of chicken into the toaster oven for seven minutes. The biggest joke is that when we bought our house, it came with this enormous double oven that has eight burners, a separate broiler, and a griddle surface. When Julia Childs died and the news showed clips from her old cooking show, I happened to notice in the background that she had the *very same oven*. Meanwhile, we've lived here for almost six years and I've used that oven exactly six times—to reheat the Thanksgiving turkey that I order every year from the gourmet market down the street. But anyway, back to dinnertime.

Chaos Level One is this: my husband and I are both picky eaters, and we're picky about different things, so even if I did cook, trying to make the same thing for him and for me is nearly impossible. My daughter, who is four, is on a weekly rotation of mac and cheese, grilled cheese, chicken tenders, and cheese tortellini with no sauce. My son, who is nineteen months, will eat only what she's having, plus spaghetti and meatballs. So on any given night, we are all eating at least three different meals that I have not made.

Which brings me to Chaos Level Two: my son gets hungry at five, so he eats by himself in his highchair in the kitchen while I ignore him and attempt to catch up on some work phone calls. My daughter gets hungry around six, so she eats at the kitchen table by herself (well, not really by herself, if you count her good friends on whatever TV show she's watching), while I ignore her and my son as I try to check my e-mail. My husband gets home around seven, and after we put the kids to bed he usually goes and picks up something from one of four chain restaurants in our neighborhood. Then he eats standing up at the kitchen counter while he goes through the mail, and I eat sitting down at the table while I read the paper. Nice.

And then there's Chaos Level Three, which is occurring inside my body and giving me a colitive ulcer because I am so stressed out about that fact that we never eat as a family—that my kids have never known a home-cooked meal, that I am setting them up for a lifetime of obesity from eating in front of the television, not to mention a lifetime of high blood pressure, heart disease, and God knows what else from all of the pesticide and trans-fat-laden crap that I allow them to eat, that I am not giving them any flax seed oil or wheat germ. All because I was too busy working for a living to ever set a good example and am still too busy working for a living to take control of the situation and get them eating right while I still have a fighting chance.

And the worst part is that I have no moral for this story, no witty solution, no answer that I have come up with at two in the morning when I am supposed to be sleeping but am instead lying wide awake, thinking about all of the ways in which I am ruining my children's lives. The only remotely satisfying solution is to remind myself that I can't do everything. I can't be a mother and a wife and volunteer at preschool and schlep my kids around to ballet classes and swim lessons and open-play-with-some-guitar-singing-at-the-end classes and go to the gym and write a book and write a column and go to the market and do laundry and feed my dog and have friends and set play dates and plan birthday parties and remember to make doctors' appointments and dentist appointments and, on top of all of that, get dinner on the table for four people all at the same time every single night and also bake muffins with flax seed oil and wheat germ in them. I just can't. And so I'm going to have to deal with this issue later. Later, when my kids are older, and hopefully, more amenable to eating chicken that isn't breaded and fried, and when they go to bed at an hour that isn't still considered daytime by many people. And when that time comes, we'll eat healthy food together, as a family, at one table, in one place. Just, most likely, that place will be in a restaurant, because I'm pretty sure that I still won't have time to cook.

INSERT MARTYRED TITLE HERE

Miriam Kamin WOULDA COULDA SHOULDA

Any veteran mom is used to dodging the slings and arrows of the child who complains that she is the meanest mama ever, or that all the other mamas are better, or that she revels in making her children miserable. Most of my compadres adopt the same attitude I do when this happens: we feign great glee and comment that our dastardly plans are finally coming together! (Bonus points for a crazed glint in the eyes and fiendish hand rubbing.) I am accustomed to such ranting from my kids. Such comments truly no longer bother me in the slightest. I expect them and know they're a good indication that I'm doing my job.

So I was completely caught off guard yesterday when a seemingly innocuous comment from my daughter cut me to the quick. We were having a great morning (indeed, the entire day was lovely), and after I consented to perhaps the third in a series of granted requests, Chickadee hugged me and then ran off, calling to her brother.

"Monkey! Come quick! Mama's being *nice* today!"

I closed myself in my bathroom and fought back tears.

I'm able to completely shrug off being called mean, but hearing my daughter sound so *surprised* that I'm being "nice" reduces me to hopeless melancholy.

I can assure myself until the cows come home that my children will grow up understanding what I've done for them, but that doesn't necessarily make it true. Maybe what's making the biggest impression in their little heads is that I say no a lot.

My job is to raise them the best way I know how, and I'm trying to do that. I don't want to be the kind of parent who places greater importance on their kids' *wants* than on their long-term *needs*. Do I hope that when all is said and done and they are grown and on their own that we'll discover friendship with one another? Absolutely. Do I think being their buddy at this point is the goal? Nope. Do I expect them to appreciate or even understand the sacrifices being made for them? Not really.

Maybe, when Chickadee said that, if I'd had a mate here to chuckle and rib me about it, I would've shrugged it off. If I had a partner in this parenting thing—a bit of perspective and a bit of support— maybe I wouldn't, in my darker moments, worry that all the kids are processing is "Daddy is fun" and "Mama makes us do chores." I can't know for sure, of course.

(Also, I can hear that vein bulging in my ex's forehead from here. I'm not saying that he never does anything, or that his parenting style is wrong. We have, in recent times, managed to come together productively on issues concerning the kids when we need to. But none of this changes the facts that 1) the kids are with me most of the time, and 2) I am much stricter than he is. This is aside from the fact that his parenting style is wrong.)

I did not set out to be a single mother. It's harder than having an in-house coparent, of course, in the purely logistical sense. Over the last few years I think I've largely adapted to a point in which there's very little about it that seems any harder than it ought to be. I've hit my groove, and things are pretty good around here. For *them*.

For me, the longer I'm on my own, the more keenly I feel the loss of having someone around to reassure me that I'm doing it right, to help me recharge when I'm worn out, to remind me that a declaration that I'm "being nice" does not necessarily indicate an assumption that I'm usually a bitch. I don't need a coparent as much as I need someone who helps take care of *me* after I spend 90 percent of my time taking care of the kids.

Also, I would like my own personal leprechaun who periodically slides down his rainbow, chucks gold coins at me, and tells me to buy myself something pretty.

Anyway. It was a moment, and it passed. We went about our day—out with friends, running errands, walking up and down the aisles at the local craft store puzzling out a project that Chickadee's working on and deciding what materials we'd need—and had a great time. Today we had a pajama day in the white glow of this morning's blizzard, and by the time supper rolled around, we were in our familiar routine. I chopped lettuce and tomatoes while Monkey wandered into the kitchen, sniffing at the air with a distrustful expression on his face and peering into the skillet on the stove.

"Why do you always make things for dinner that I *hate*?" he whined. I clenched my teeth and pointed out that he *likes* tacos, that in fact I had chosen tacos *because* I know it's something that he likes, and that I try very hard to make a nice dinner every night, and—I stopped.

"I make things for dinner that you hate because I'm trying to kill you," I told him. His whines turned to reluctant giggles as I kissed his neck.

"I like tacos, Mama," piped up Chickadee. "In fact I like *everything* that you make for dinner." Her sucking up earned her a kiss and a squeeze as I slid past her to put milk on the table. And then she and I enjoyed our dinner while Monkey blew bubbles into his milk and whined until I excused him. Afterward, he cleaned up in the playroom while Chickadee helped me with the dishes. Later, we all read together, and I tucked them both into their beds and bid them goodnight.

It's OK. They're OK. It's only me who's not.

Miriam Kamin remarried in the spring of 2007 and is still the heavy with her kids, but she doesn't mind as much as she used to.

WHO THE HELL DO I THINK I AM?

Jennifer Satterwhite MOMMY NEEDS COFFEE

I once received a nasty little e-mail from someone, a stranger, no less, who confronted me about a project I had in the works. In the e-mail the person asked me, in quite the nasty way, *"Who the hell do you think you are to do this?"* My first instinct was to fire off my own response pretty much questioning that person's parentage and telling them where to go and how to get there. But calmer heads prevailed, and I kept quiet.

But it really did get me thinking. "Who the hell *am* I?"

Well, I am a wife and mother. A sister and daughter. A niece. An aunt. A cousin. A friend. Those are a few of my labels. Those are easy. But that doesn't answer the question of who I am.

I cry when I hold a newborn.

I laugh at the silly and the immature things in life.

I get angry when someone kicks the underdog.

My attention span is short but my patience is long.

My feelings can get hurt too easily but my will is strong.

If I love you I do so with all of my heart.

Friendship means everything to me.

If you cross me I won't hold back in letting you know how I feel. By the same token, when I appreciate you I won't hold back my gratitude either.

So, "Who the hell *am* I?"

I am that eighth-grade girl whose best friend became her worst enemy in a matter of days for reasons that were never clear to her, so she always blamed herself. The young girl who will always have a part of her think it is *her* fault now when a friendship goes south.

I am that sixteen-year-old teen who immediately had a crush on that sixteen-year-old boy at a high school party. The girl who blushed every time that boy looked at her. That sixteen-year-old girl who *still* blushes when that boy she married looks at her that way after all these years together.

I am a woman in her mid-thirties who still feels like she is playing house when she talks to her friends about mortgages, parenting, and the best school districts. A woman who wonders at what age she will finally feel like a legitimate adult.

I am a daughter who is watching her mother be destroyed by a disease that has no cure, no chance of improvement, and does nothing but destroy. The daughter who still wants to crawl into her mother's lap and have her make it all better but finds herself doing all of the comforting in their relationship.

I am a mother whose baby died way too soon. A mother who is raising her three children, but still says a prayer on her son's birthday. A mother who will always hold a spot in her heart for all four of her children.

I am a mother who does her best to raise her children without screwing them up too much. A mother who questions most parental decisions, yet still watches her children thrive in spite of it all. A mother who tries to find her own way as a parent, yet still falls back on the lessons learned from her own childhood.

I am a drug addict who fights daily the battle to make the right choices when I am under immense stress. I try not to take the easy way out. I am an addict who, when she feels backed into a corner, can easily forget how bad it can get but quickly can recall how good it felt. But an addict who is five years clean, nevertheless.

I am a writer who puts her heart into her words and (even when she gets paid for her work) still wonders if she has any talent. A writer who tries to ignore the critics, yet hears their voices the loudest.

I am all of those things and so much more. Want to try to slam me down by asking me who the hell I think *I am*? Bring it on. I'd be more than happy to tell you.

THE MENOPAUSAL HUT
Grace Davis STATE OF GRACE

The idea that I would be severely felled (like bedridden felled) by the wildly fluctuating hormones of menopause is an odd notion, indeed. But, folks, it's happening: I am *exhausted*. For those who have hung out with me at latte fueling stations, patiently listening to my caffeine-driven rants and raves, it is easier to imagine that my estrogen storm would prompt hollering at the wind, if not the kid, the hubs, and, of course, the Radical Religious Right. Well, I do that too. Ask Molly and her friends. Recently, I committed the dire and ultimate parental sin of yelling at not only Molly, but her entire girl posse. The exact tirade is a blur to me. All I remember is getting out of bed at 11:00 P.M. to drive them from A to B, then they wanted to go to Burger King, where I had to do the dreaded thing—use the drive-through. Who hates having six teenagers holler out their complicated fast-food orders past her ear and out the driver's window? I do! I do! Hell, we all do! Thus, it was logical at that moment to screech, "WHY DIDN'T YOU GUYS EAT BEFORE THE MOVIES? WHY? WHY? WHY?"

I know, irrational and dangerous. Estrogen Terrorism.

Time to descend down the wooded path to my Menopausal Hut, which is not a house of banishment or detention, but a middle-aged woman's retreat. The Menopausal Hut is pleasant, with sunlit, airy rooms and a full bathroom complete with a Japanese furo soaking tub. There's an efficient little kitchen with a nifty electric whistling kettle for tea and a glass jar full of Snickerdoodle cookies. Books are plentiful, as are magazines, mostly the good, cheesy ones, like *People* and its tawdry cousin, *US Weekly*.

There's a feather bed. Ahhhhh! Feather duvet. Oooooo! And ten feather pillows. Mmmm!

I tucked myself in with a *People* magazine (Jennifer Aniston on the cover), brewed up some chamomile tea, then took a luxurious soak in the furo bath. I recovered nicely and was able to pull myself together in time to take the kiddo out for a mother-daughter brunch.

At the table, Moll was distant and apologized for it. "I'm sorry I'm killing brunch, Mom."

"I know you're upset with me for yelling at you and your friends," I said, taking a bite of Crow Pie.

"Yeah. You know, you can yell at me, but don't yell at my friends, please."

I yammered just a little bit, I swear, just a teeny tiny bit, about the drive-through window business, but then stopped myself to have another slice o' crow.

"Oh, I understand. And I apologize, honey. I really, really do. And I'll apologize to your friends. Your old mom is tired these days. Menopause is kicking my butt. However, I should have known better."

I almost blurted out that I could make it up to the girls by driving them down to Disneyland and Universal Studios for a weekend, but the dessert tray showed up and I shut the fuck up.

So I'm back at the keyboard. I will answer my e-mail. I will call my friends. I will do the 4:30 P.M. yoga practice today.

I will be a better mother.

And I will ask my hubs, very nicely and wearing my laciest camisole, if we could build a Menopausal Hut sometime very soon. Because what I described above was a total figment of my imagination. But you were right there in the furo bath with me, weren't you?

10

This Is Motherhood

It's hard to write on the subject of motherhood without sounding corny. There's nothing I hate more than e-mail addresses like "calebsmom4ever@yahoo.com." Yes, it's true, having a baby rips out your heart, trots it around the block, and stuffs it back inside your body rode hard and put away wet. It's true, everything your child accomplishes engenders a pride heretofore inconceivable. It's also true that nobody else wants to hear about it, except maybe your significant other and both sets of grandparents. Knowing that nobody else cares about your child's life as much as you do can be heartbreaking or empowering, depending on how you look at it. But as Eden Marriott Kennedy says in her essay, *this is motherhood*. It's a very personal journey for each of us. Own your experience. It's one of the few things in life uniquely yours.

TO BE OR NOT TO BE, THAT IS THE QUESTION

Amy Jo Jones BINKYTOWN

My obstetrician was about to have her second child, her second in twelve months. That rattles my brain just thinking about it.

When I told her I admired her stamina, being ready again so soon, she laughed it off, saying, "If I weren't going to be thirty-nine when this baby is born . . . I really wanted more kids, but it was either two back-to-back or one, and we chose two, so here I am."

This is the doctor who comforted me after my first miscarriage. Who eased my fears during my second pregnancy by telling me that there was a 98 percent chance for a healthy pregnancy after hearing the baby's heartbeat. (A number which became my mantra in those days and nights when every twinge filled me with anxiety: 98 percent, 98 percent . . .)

She assured me at my last visit that at thirty-five, I have plenty (and she did stress plenty) of time to have another baby. To not feel like I should rush if I weren't ready. If she was telling me this, of course it must be true. She's a doctor—a pregnant, thirty-nine-year-old OB. She knows what she's talking about.

She lost her second baby at twenty-four weeks. Preterm labor. The baby survived for four days.

I don't know if she knew it was going to happen, or if she had an existing medical condition of some kind that predisposed her to this outcome. Maybe she was exhausted from the demands of being a mother and a wife and an OB who worked around the clock on little sleep or sustenance. Maybe it was all too much. Maybe it wasn't, and it would have happened anyway, even if she were twenty-nine, because it wasn't meant to be and you can't reason with your uterus.

This is the part of motherhood, of pregnancy and beyond, that really scares me. The fact that you can't control any of it. Once the cells start dividing, it's out of your hands. That's a hard thing to accept.

I don't know if this means anything other than simply illustrating that life is not fair, but it has me wondering—am I doing the wrong thing by waiting? Does waiting put a future pregnancy at greater risk? Her answer the first time I asked that question was no. I wonder what she would say now. I believed her when she told me I had a 98 percent chance for a successful pregnancy. I felt such relief when she told me I had plenty of time to try again. I have such faith in her. If it were anybody but her I would have thought, you never know, anything could go wrong. But I trusted her. The way she must have trusted her body, and it let her down.

How do you weigh the choice when it's all so random? I could have another baby now. My risk for developmental delays or complications is lower than it would be two or three years from now, but would it break me? Create an anxious pregnancy? Put further strain on my marriage? Our financial situation? Take away from the child we already have? If we wait until we can better afford it and I feel ready to do the diapers and the sleepless nights and the pumping, am I taking too big of a chance? Creating an anxious pregnancy? Increasing my risk of delays and complications? Would that break me? Put a huge strain on my marriage?

The reality is that if I want to have another baby, I need to be willing to accept what comes. Maybe I'll miscarry again. Maybe I'll have complications. Maybe I will have a child with a developmental delay. This is the truth, no matter what your doctor tells you. I just wish she didn't have to go through this for me to realize it.

THIS IS MOTHERHOOD

Eden Marriott Kennedy FUSSY

Back when I was pregnant, I found it impossible to imagine what having a baby around all the time would really be like. I hadn't planned on becoming pregnant—indeed, I'd never imagined myself to be mother material at all—so I didn't have a lifetime of preparation that some women seem to get, starting with diapering their baby brothers and sisters and moving on through babysitting, baby showers, Pottery Barn catalogs, etc. And having strangers come up to me, pat my belly, and say, "Get your sleep now, while you can!" was irritating, not instructional.

Nobody can really tell you what it's like, but for every child-free person who has ever wondered "*what's the big deal?*" I have developed this simple visualization exercise. Find a comfortable seated position, close your eyes, take a deep breath, and we'll begin.

- Imagine you have a roommate.
- A roommate who communicates in cries, grunts, laughter, and blank stares.
- A roommate who needs you to carry him everywhere.
- Who grabs the remote out of your hand when you're watching television and then starts randomly selecting channels and volume levels.
- Who needs to be dressed, sometimes three or four times a day, because he pukes on himself.

- Who swats the cup of hot coffee out of your hand.
- Who bangs on the keyboard while you're typing.
- Who pulls your hair.
- Who falls asleep on your shoulder while you're vacuuming his room.
- Who cries when you leave him and ignores you when you come back.
- Who is so magnetic that relatives will travel thousands of miles just to ogle him, and then plead for new photographs weekly, saying, "It only takes a second, just pop some in the mail!"
- Who wakes you up at 3:30 A.M. crying or wanting to play.
- Who wakes you up at 5:30 A.M. wanting to suck on your nipples.
- Who would rather be naked than clothed.
- Who stuffs fistfuls of Cheerios into his mouth, and then coughs until he turns bright red.
- Who cries when his grandma tries to pick him up and stops crying when *you* pick him up, thereby insulting grandma in the most personal way possible.
- Whom both you and your husband love sometimes, secretly, more than each other.

EVERY NIGHT SINCE YOU WERE BORN

Rita Arens SURRENDER, DOROTHY

Dear Little Angel,

I know someday you will discover this blog, probably buried in the depths of Google, or the Search Engine Formerly Known as Google, as it will probably be by the time you learn to read.

I've bitched a lot about your sleeping, or lack thereof.

You will probably wonder why I bothered to have you if all I was going to do was complain about my lack of beauty rest. Of course, if you know me well, you will understand that I often tell stories about my life in order to put them in a better light through humor. Or what I think is humor but may some day be taken hard by you.

I'm not going to stop. I'm your mother, my love, and I'm hard-wired this way. But I do want to give you the flip side, the side I haven't chronicled in such depth.

Every night since you were born, every night that we have shared the same roof, I have crept into your bedroom before I go to sleep, sometimes (in the early days) five or six times, to touch your belly, checking for breath, and to kiss your sleepy, dreamy red head. Often you stir, turning to your side. Sometimes you mew like a kitten and grab my hand.

I can't sleep until I know you are safe and warm.

When you do wake up and cry, my first instinct, the first thought that crosses my mind, is to make sure my little girl is safe. Only once I have verified that all your limbs are still attached and your breathing is normal (if harried) do I look at the clock and groan.

Only then.

You have been an otherwise perfect child. Perfect strangers are amazed by your "no, thank yous" at the age of two-and-a-half. You are physically and emotionally beautiful, breathtaking to behold. You have had a time-out fewer than twenty times in your entire life. One day, after you ran away from me at a movie theater, you came back and reached out to hug me. "I won't let you get lost, Mommy," you said. If I give you a certain look, you come running to me with open arms. "I love you, Mommy," you say. "You are mine."

Many times when we were going through that six-month toddler period when you woke every two to three hours, I told people that perhaps every child has to have some element that tries the patience and resolve of his or her parents. Maybe yours is your delicate sleep. And though it seems odd that nature would pair a child who hates sleep with a mother who needs at least nine hours a night to feel whole and sane, I have never regretted having you or wished you would go away. I only have to think for one instant of life without you before I go running to you to say, "You are mine. I love you, Little Angel."

You are mine, and I am yours. One day I will get enough sleep, and then I will miss your sleepy, dreamy head.

Now that we're all clear, I may bitch just a little bit more about your night waking. But you know how I really feel.

Love,

Mommy

BECOMING MAMA

Karen CHEEK

When I met my daughter for the first time, she was already saying Mama, but much to my dismay it was not for me. On September 11, 2006, in a courtroom in Hefei, China, my husband and I became new parents to a thirteen-month-old baby girl. She had no idea who we were, no clue that her life was about to take a drastic turn. And all we had was a few pictures, some medical information, and a page of checkmarked boxes that told us our daughter was closest to her caregiver, slept through the night, and could eat a biscuit all by herself. There was also a box checked telling us that she said Mama already. Though we didn't talk much about it, both of us were crossing all of our fingers and toes that the Chinese government had matched us with a baby that would someday feel like ours. And though I didn't talk about it, I was hoping that within a few days, she'd be saying Mama to me.

That first day it took us a few minutes to approach our daughter. We were both terrified—even after five years of talking about being parents, once in the moment we were all awkward smiles and stiff limbs, strangers to not only our daughter, but each other and ourselves, too. Who were we, who were we about to become? We finally, tentatively, ventured over bearing gifts: toys, video camera, a new mother and father. Our daughter, who was already crying, spotted us—the interlopers. She opened her mouth, a silent baby bird. And then she let out a huge wail. Maybe she sensed something, smelled our eagerness or fear. Our daughter scrambled for her caregiver, the woman who, up until that moment, had been her mama.

"Mama," the orphanage worker said, pointing to me. "Mama." This made our daughter's eyes squeeze out an avalanche of tears. Her screams had a quality to them that was almost like growling, and she kept choking. I worried that she would strangle on her own sobs. I shook toys in our daughter's face, called her name, *Maya, Maya, Maya*, like a song, over and over, hoping to soothe her. As if she would recognize her name, recognize us. We had pictures of her and barely recognized her. I'm not sure whether I thought that she would instinctually know who we were, have a deeper knowledge of us in her blood, or something fate related like that, but we were very much strangers to each other.

Maya had a rice cracker in one hand and, despite her obvious distress, was attempting to take bites of it through her tears. She wore denim overalls and a simple white-collared shirt, nothing like the stacks of expensive baby clothes I had waiting for her in the hotel room. Everything about her seemed unfamiliar yet familiar at the same time—we knew her from pictures but had no idea who she was. What we imagined she'd be like was cobbled together from stories we had heard of other adoptions and our own hopes and dreams. But she was the most beautiful baby either of us had ever seen, even with rice cracker stuck to her chin and sobs scrunching up her face. We stood there, unsure of what to do, awkward and feeling like we were in the way. The caregiver hovered, reminding Maya that we were her parents. I think we needed some reminding too.

I was afraid to pick up my daughter. I didn't know how to comfort her, since I was the thing making her so upset. I didn't know how to be her mother. I had waited five years to arrive at this moment, through countless infertility treatments and surgeries, canceled hopes, and adoption paperwork that many times made me cry from the sheer weight of it. Becoming a mother was all I wanted. I listed "getting pregnant" as a hobby on an Internet board I joined for support in conceiving. I charted my cycles for months, tracking my basal temperature every morning religiously on charts I kept in a binder. I peed on so many sticks I joked about taking out stock in the company. Nothing worked. I was never pregnant. The word "negative" started to mean more than just a sign on a home pregnancy test; it became synonymous for all of the things missing from my life, the literal minus, the baby and life I was forced to do without.

I felt negative space fill my empty womb as each month passed and first Plan A, then Plan B, then Plan H went out the window. I went to therapy. I lost friends who were mothers because I was so jealous of what they had. I looked at mothers in the supermarket and glared at them: how dare they parade their motherhood? A woman in line at a checkout counter offered me her twin boys as a joke. I said nothing, but my heart turned over, basted in a bitter syrup. I was angry, depressed, and full of a dark fog that I could only hope would dissipate once I finally became a mother.

And in China I finally, on paper, officially became a mother.

But in the hotel room with Maya, I felt as if I were babysitting. It felt surreal—nothing belonged to me there, everything felt strange. It was hard to feel as if this new child belonged to me. And once home with Maya, I still did not feel entirely like a mother, although I went through all of the motions. At night, my daughter raged in my arms, her body stiff and arched away from me. She pushed my hands away if I tried to hold her. I hung on to the idea that she would love me, eventually, and magic would follow. I read attachment books, learned how to help my daughter bond, and went through the suggestions. We bathed together, we played together, I did everything for her—fed her, changed her diaper, put her to sleep. I resisted help from family. I walked with her in a sling, close to me.

And the whole time I wondered: When will I attach? When will I feel like a real mother, and, more importantly, *her* mother? I hung all of my hopes on that single word: *Mama*. It started to take on mythical proportions. I imagined my daughter looking up at me, love like a clear day in her face, saying Mama as she slipped her arms around my neck. Maya babbled the word "mama" over and over, but it didn't mean anything; it was just a fun sound to say. I felt sure that once she was able to say it—and know who it belonged to— that I would *finally* feel like Mama. I was waiting for my daughter to name, and claim, me as her mother.

In the outside world, people stared at us. A blonde, white woman with a Chinese daughter, especially one as cute as ours, seemed a novelty for some folks. People did double takes; some had no expression, some had a sour look, and some smiled in a way that made me wince. People told me what a saint I was (for having a beautiful daughter? No. Anyone would be lucky to have her). People questioned our relationship all the time. "Are you babysitting?" one store clerk asked. "No, I'm her mother," I responded. "Oh, adopted?" the clerk asked, as if it mattered.

I didn't *want* to qualify our relationship that way—Maya is my daughter who happens to be adopted, not my adopted daughter. But the world demanded clarification. And ironically, so did I. I couldn't just be a mom; Maya couldn't just be my daughter. And it did matter that she was adopted, because it meant that I couldn't depend on the clean slate of a newborn. I had entered into her life at thirteen months, not at birth. I had missed essential moments. And as the world questioned whether or not I was Maya's mother, I did, too.

I'm not sure when the change started to happen. Sometime after she had been at home for five weeks, we fell into a predictable routine. Maya started responding to me more; in turn, I responded to her in more loving ways. Our attachment seemed to be strengthening. She raged less, and then not at all. She began walking, then running through the house, and one day she fell and hit the corner of her eye on an un-baby-proofed table and cried on my shoulder for five minutes. (I went out the next day to get soft covers.) I marveled at how I was able to stop her tears, how I felt confident that I could comfort her.

Maya reached for me constantly but began venturing out on her own also, giving me some space. She learned how to give kisses. She became delirious with excitement in the mornings when I would come to retrieve her from her crib. I began to feel something stir, a great fog break up. As she grew confident in public, so did I. When people stared, I smiled—look, *look* at my beautiful daughter. Her firsts were, in many ways, my firsts as well.

The other day we were taking a walk. It was a beautiful day. Maya was in her stroller, babbling happily, almost singing. And she started saying "Mama, Mama," over and over, and patting her chest as she said it—the same way I say "Mama" and pat my chest. "No, silly!" I bent down to look at her in the stroller, and she grinned at me. "I'm Mama!" I said.

Maya patted herself again and said, "Mama!"

And in that moment, I realized I knew who I was. "I'm Mama!" I said again, laughing. I didn't need her to say that I was her mama anymore, because we both knew it. Somewhere in all of that work, it had happened. It's in the way she curls her arms around my neck when I pick her up, the way she rubs her forehead on mine and then gives me an openmouthed kiss on the nose, the way she squawks when I don't pay her enough attention. It took a lot of tears and hard work on both our parts, but we finally know who we are: mother and daughter, at last.

WHAT HAVE I DONE?

Izzy Dean IZZYMOM

On any given day it wouldn't be unusual, if you could read my mind, to hear me asking myself, "What have I done?" This would be a reference to my children and the fact that we decided to have another one when the first one was four and becoming very independent. Now I'm up to my ears in obscene amounts of laundry, diapers, baby food, bottles, and nursing pads that seem to end up all over the house— occasionally stuck to my ass. As if that weren't enough to handle, my son is teething and cranky, and lately he seems to never sleep.

My daughter, who has become quite an amazing little girl, is a handful in other ways. For one thing, a mess seems to follow her wherever she's been. I used to be able to help her pick up but now I always have a baby in my arms. Nagging her to do it herself is exhausting in its own right. The end result is that my once mostly tidy house has become a torrent of toys, baby items, and my own clutter that I don't seem to be able to catalog, or the time to even try.

My daughter also talks a lot. This is not at all uncommon for her age. Every mother of a five-year-old will tell you the same thing, but for me it's like sensory overload sometimes. The baby is fussing or crying or saying his new favorite word—dadadadadada, which may or may not be his version of "Daddy"—my daughter is happily chattering, singing, or humming endlessly, and usually some toy or other thing is making noise or music. Is it any mystery that I'm so grouchy sometimes?

Before you write me off as just another miserable stay-at-home-mom, I do, thankfully, have other thoughts, pleasant ones even.

For example, I'm frequently thinking how much I love these two beings. No matter how stressful motherhood is or how tired I am or how much I long for peace and sleep and a clean house, my love for them prevails and trumps everything else. They are so beautiful and so perfect in every imaginable way. I swear to God they emanate light. Every smile, every moment of shared silliness, and every hug reinforces my belief that I have, in fact, made the right choices in life.

If you could see how much my children love each other, it would make you tear up. My daughter is so protective of, so kind, too, and so patient with her baby brother. He gazes at her and follows her every move. He grins with absolute glee when she walks into the room. I never dreamed that I would witness this much love between them. I honestly thought she would be terribly jealous of him, but she's not. She seems to intuitively understand that he needs more of my attention and that my love for her is not diminished in the least by my love for him. I told you she was amazing.

My son, equally enchanting, is now clapping his hands and waving bye-bye. I'm certain I've never seen anything more endearing and precious. Everyday I fall in love with him all over again.

And it's because these children bring me closer to pure love than anything else in my entire life that I know it's OK to occasionally ask, "What have I done?" The answer is in their eyes.

SHOULD I HAVE TOLD HER?

Kelli Oliver George RANCID RAVES

I have a friend who is going into the hospital tonight to be induced/ helped along with the delivery of her baby. She isn't due yet, but she is going early because of her gall bladder. Hands down, this has been one of the most difficult pregnancies I have witnessed. So to say that she is "ready for this baby to just get here already" is a bit of an understatement. When I talked to her last night, I just felt like I had *so* many things to tell her, bits of "assvice," things to share. I remember my own last days in mid-October last year, standing on the precipice of one of the biggest journeys of my life. The excitement. The anticipation. The gut-wrenching fear. However, I tried to keep my pearls of mothering wisdom to myself. After all, isn't that part of the fun? Discovering all the wonders for yourself? But here's what I would have liked to tell her.

That when you first see your baby you might be so pumped up on drugs and adrenaline that it might not be like one of those scenes from all the movies and television. You may be shell shocked and think, "Wow, what a sweet, adorable baby. She's mine? For real?"

That bonding with your child is a lifelong process. It doesn't happen just because you breastfeed or hold her or kiss her or wipe her butt or carry her in a sling 24/7 or co-sleep with her. It's a lifetime of shared experiences beginning with many of those things I just mentioned.

That you can never, ever take too many pictures of your baby.

That you will feel so vulnerable and exposed when you realize exactly how much of your heart is wrapped up in your daughter. It may even terrify you. Furthermore, you will have to swallow the frustration over the fact that you can't completely protect her from every disaster.

That sometimes in the wee hours of the morning you will doubt your love, but you shouldn't dwell on it or feel guilty about it because 8:00 A.M. is just around the corner and somehow, someway, love gets a boost at precisely that hour.

That breastfeeding is one of the most painful, frustrating, yet ultimately wondrous experiences you can have with your baby.

That taking a nap curled up with your baby is a peaceful calm like no other. Also? Having one cat curled up in your knees and another against your back is just gooey icing.

That taking a shower, putting on a minimum of makeup, and wearing decent clothes *every day* is crucial to your self-esteem. Letting your appearance go by the wayside is a slippery slope that is best avoided.

That you may look at many of your former hobbies with a casual, detached curiosity. Like, "Hmmmm, I used to actually *have time* to count stitches and rows? I'm lucky to get a scarf done these days." Don't fret over lost hobbies—you'll have time for all of them again someday. Just pick the most important ones for the time being.

That being a good mother is all about ideas, not answers. Get ideas from *all* of your friends, then mix and match according to *your* baby.

That some baby topics are best left un-Googled.

That in the beginning, you will want to change her outfits several times a day because she is just *too damned cute* in all of them.

That your relationship with your husband will change and morph into something that it's never been. You will see sides of each other that you never knew existed, but this doesn't have to be a bad thing.

That in the first few weeks it's best to unapologetically focus on yourself and your baby.

That when you *are* healed 100 percent, you should try to get out of the house every single day. Even if it is just to pick up bread or milk. Damned straight, sitting in a house all day with a baby can do a serious number on your mental health.

That it is imperative to surround yourself with good mothering examples—the sort of gals that are *good* for your mothering self-esteem, the sort of gals who don't *compare* and don't *compete*. If you find yourself in a group that compares and competes, get the fuck *out*. Stat.

That just when you think you have it all figured out, your baby will change the rules. And will give little to no warning.

That ultimately, *you know your baby best*. Can I say that again, for effect? You know your baby *best*. Also, notice that I said she is *your* baby. So gracefully accept advice, wrap your brain around it, put it in your back pocket for later consideration, and then do what *you feel comfortable doing*. This will sometimes even include your doctor. And often your mother-in-law.

That even the darkest of days are worth it for the moments when your sweet child snuggles her head deep under your chin. And then *both* of you find a peaceful calm like no other.

INDEX OF CONTRIBUTOR BLOGS

Amalah

www.amalah.com

Amy Corbett Storch is a freelance writer and semiprofessional blogger in Washington, D.C., whose humorous adventures in pregnancy, motherhood, and other disasters can be found in her blog, Amalah. She started the site in 2003 when she was a childless urbanite with too many handbags. She has been featured in *The Washingtonian* and has made Technorati's top ten searches. She also writes the Advice Smackdown column for Alpha Mom and is the cofounder of Mamapop.

Binkytown

http://amywojo.typepad.com

Amy Jo Jones lives with her family in Milwaukee, Wisconsin. She is a graduate of the University of Wisconsin–Milwaukee with a degree in English and a minor in women's studies. She was nominated for a Perfect Post award in 2007.

Birdie's New Mexico Time Machine

http://birdiejaworski.com

Birdie Jaworksi writes a weekly human interest column for the *Las Vegas Times*. Her writing has appeared in many online and print journals. Her former blog, Beauty Dish, was featured in the *New York Times, Time Magazine,* and the *Wall Street Journal.* Birdie Jaworski lives in the high desert, a delighted transplant to the Land of Enchantment. Her two boys are growing too fast.

Cheek
http://thenakedovary.typepad.com/cheek
Karen wrote The Naked Ovary until choosing to end the blog in 2006. The Naked Ovary was included in *Blogosphere: Best of Blogs* (Peter Kuhns and Adrienne Crew). After battling infertility, she and her husband adopted their daughter in 2006. Karen restarted blogging at Cheek in 2007. Her work will soon appear in an anthology for Love Without Boundaries.

CityMama
http://citymama.com
Stefania Pomponi Butler is a writer and blog producer/editor. She likes sunsets, long walks on the beach, and children who don't act a fool. Stefania is obsessed with pop culture, flat-ironing, karaoke, and moisturization. Her work has appeared on AOL, NPR, ABC-News.com and in the *New York Times.* In addition to writing her personal blogs, CityMama and Family Food, Stefania has also blogged for Strollerderby and is a contributing editor to BlogHer. She lives in Silicon Valley, California, with her husband (and his pile of laundry), their two impossibly cute (and very loud) girls, and about 2,649 plastic horses.

Finslippy

http://finslippy.typepad.com

Alice Bradley, her husband, and her son used to live in Brooklyn, but they now live in New Jersey. Although they do miss the vermin, they're adjusting to their new lifestyle. Alice Bradley's work has been published in several literary journals. Her blog, Finslippy, has been featured in the *New York Times* and was nominated in 2006 for a Bloggie Award. She spoke on the mommyblogging panel at the 2006 BlogHer conference and also authors Wonderland for Alpha Mom.

Friday Playdate

http://fridayplaydate.com

Once upon a time, not so very long ago, Susan Wagner taught literature in a fabulous liberal studies program near Seattle, spending days pondering the origins of the novel, the relationship between gender and genre, and the impact of colonialism on the postmodern narrative. Now she lives in Oklahoma City with her husband and two young sons (Henry and Charlie), passing the time contemplating which superhero is the strongest, which park has the most shade, and how many ways vegetarian chicken nuggets can be garnished. She also writes Friday Playdate, which was featured in the magazines *Nichols Hills News, Norman Living*, and *NW Style*. She writes a media column for Mamazine.com and is a contributor for BlogHer and Blogging Baby.

Fussy

www.fussy.org

Eden Marriott Kennedy has been blogging since the birth of her son in 2001. Fussy has been featured in the *New York Times*, the *San Francisco Chronicle*, and the *Newark Star-Ledger*. She lives with her husband, son, and beloved dogs in southern California.

IzzyMom

http://izzymom.com

Izzy Dean is a married and largely undomestic work-at-home mom of a boy and a girl. She writes IzzyMom and contributes to Cool Mom Picks, Mamapop, Blogger Chicks, and 9 Rules. Her work has also been published on the Huffington Post. She resides, reluctantly, in Florida but hopes to someday live somewhere more progressive. Until then she continues to bide her time by searching locally for intelligent life, buttwiping, carpooling, avoiding hurricanes, and thinking of ways to get out of cooking dinner for her very patient and understanding family.

Laid-off Dad

http://laidoffdad.typepad.com

Doug French's two favorite pastimes are writing and being a dad. After he lost his job in 2003, he started his blog, Laid-Off Dad, to find humor among the stress and penury. Then *Parents* magazine found him, a few newspapers interviewed him, and readers chose LOD as the Best Daddy Blog in the Best of Blogs awards for 2005. Currently biding his time between layoffs, Doug lives in New York City. He is the only man to appear in this anthology. Which is surely indicative of something.

The Modernity Ward

http://leerypolyp.blogs.com/the_modernity_ward

Joanna Polyn is underemployed, mother to Sophia, married to her own personal scientist, and living in Philadelphia with a view of the oil refineries. Her blog was featured in the book *Blogosphere: The Best of Blogs* (Peter Kuhns and Adrienne Crew) and was nominated for a Perfect Post award in 2006.

Mom-101

http://mom-101.blogspot.com

Liz Gumbinner wears many hats, from award-winning creative director to published author and columnist to mom blogger. Mom-101 has garnered attention from the *New York Times* and the *Minneapolis Star-Tribune*. She's also the editor of the shopping review site Cool Mom Picks. When not on the computer, Liz can be found slumming it in Brooklyn with her partner, Nate, their two daughters, and a very stubborn English Bulldog.

Mommy Needs Coffee

www.mommyneedscoffee.com

Jennifer Satterwhite is a native Texan living in the Dallas area with her geek-proud husband of seventeen years, two sons, one daughter, and ninety-pound Doberman (who thinks he is a lapdog). Mommy Needs Coffee has been featured on the nationally syndicated radio show *Kidd Kraddick in the Morning* and in a nationally syndicated television news segment on mommyblogging. She spends her free time tormenting the local PTA (as she serves among them) and chauffeuring her three children around town to soccer, gymnastics, and any other over-scheduled activity they can sign up for.

Mommy Track'd

http://mommytrackd.com/features/risagreen

Risa Green is a critically acclaimed author who lives in Los Angeles. In the last four years, she has produced two children, Harper and Davis, and two novels, *Notes from the Underbelly* and *Tales from the Crib*. *Notes from the Underbelly* became the basis of a television series for ABC.

Motherhood Uncensored

http://motherhooduncensored.typepad.com

Kristen Chase is a Yankee living in Atlanta after just barely surviving a year-long stint with her in-laws. Prior to finding herself knee-deep as a parent of two young children, Kristen was a published textbook author, musician, college professor, and designer shoe glutton, all of which she's traded for a satisfying new position as military wife and stay-at-home parent. She's the author of Motherhood Uncensored, a no-holds-barred mom blog, and also the cofounder of Parent Bloggers Network, the other half of Cool Mom Picks, and a sex columnist for parents (as the "Mominatrix").

Not Calm (dot com)

http://notcalmdotcom.typepad.com

Jenifer Scharpen began writing Not Calm (dot com) in July of 2002. An eighth-generation Texan living in northern California, she has a hard time making up her mind about a lot of things, but she does know the value of a hard day's work, a good night's sleep, and long conversations that take place in the kitchen.

Paper Napkin

http://papernapkin.typepad.com

Sheryl Patten is the author of *Paper Napkin*, which is among Technorati's top five parenting blogs. She lives with her husband and three children in Ohio.

Rancid Raves

http://rancidraves.blogspot.com

Kelli Oliver George has been blogging since 2004. Until the birth of her son in 2005, she held various positions in the workplace, including CPA, auditor, business systems analyst, and data security analyst. Her blog, Rancid Raves, details the rise of her career as she threw away nearly twenty years of education in one fell swoop to stay home full-time with her son and daughter.

State of Grace

http://gracedavis.typepad.com

Born in 1955, Grace Davis may be the oldest mommyblogger on the World Wide Web. However, Grace insists on maintaining hip and cool creds with reluctant guidance from her biokid daughter and five grown stepkids. Her blog, State of Grace, has been featured in the *New York Times*. She has spoken on panels at the South by Southwest Interactive Media Festival and was on the keynote panel at the 2006 BlogHer conference. Grace is a contributing editor for BlogHer and also serves on the advisory board.

Surfette

http://surfette.typepad.com

Lisa Stone has launched popular communities and interactive programming for many national brands, including BlogHer, Women. com (acquired by iVillage), Hearst and Rodale magazines, E! Television/Online, HBO's *Sex and the City*, Gallup, Bloomberg, Law.com, and Glam.com. Lisa also has written for the *New York Times, Los Angeles Times,* CNN, and the *Oakland Tribune,* among other publications. She is the first Internet journalist awarded a Nieman Fellowship by Harvard University. Lisa lives in the San Francisco Bay area with Christopher Carfi and their children.

Surrender, Dorothy
http://surrenderdorothyblog.com
(Editor) Rita Arens grew up in small-town Iowa as Rita Biermann, a pen name she only recently dropped. She moved to Kansas City via Chicago in 1998 and now lives there with her husband and daughter. Her fiction, poetry, and magazine articles have appeared in eleven newspapers, magazines, and journals. Her blog, Surrender, Dorothy, has been featured in the *Kansas City Star, Austin American Statesmen, Businessweek online,* Silicon Valley Moms Blog, Mommybloggers, and Guy Kawasaki's list of ultimate mommybloggers. She is a contributing editor in BlogHer's mommy and family category, coauthors She Doesn't Get It, and writes Surrender Dorothy: Reviews.

Sweetney
www.sweetney.com
Tracey Gaughran-Perez writes Sweetney. She lives in Baltimore with her husband and daughter. Prior to marriage and domesticity, she was a graduate student in English literature for most of her adult life. Remaining in school forever allowed her to delay her entry into responsible adulthood while simultaneously gaining really useful,

practical knowledge of things like continental philosophy, decon-structivist theory, and the ravages of postmodernism. Despite all this, she is indeed still fun at parties. She was a speaker at the 2006 BlogHer conference and at the 2007 South by Southwest Interactive.

Three Kid Circus
http://threekidcircus.com/ threekidcircus
Jenny Lauck writes Three Kid Circus and is the cofounder of Mommy bloggers.com. She was a speaker at BlogHer 2005 and was a con-tributor to Club Mom. Jenny lives with her husband and three chil-dren in northern California.

Woulda Coulda Shoulda
http://wouldashoulda.com
Miriam Kamin is a freelance writer from New England who has been mothering since 1998 and blogging since 2004. She now lives with her husband and two children in Georgia. Her personal blog, Woulda Coulda Shoulda, has been featured as a Yahoo! Pick of the Day and a Feedster Feed of the day, as well as being highlighted in *Blogosphere: Best of Blogs* (Que, 2006) and the April 2007 issue of *Parents* magazine. She is a regular columnist for parenting sites such as Maya's Mom and Work It, Mom!, and is a contributing editor to BlogHer in the mommy and family category.